Macbeth

ARDEN STUDENT SKILLS: LANGUAGE AND WRITING

Series Editor:
Dympna Callaghan
Syracuse University

Published Titles
The Tempest: Language and Writing, Brinda Charry
Macbeth: Language and Writing, Emma Smith

Forthcoming Titles
Hamlet, Dympna Callaghan
Othello, Laurie Maguire
Twelfth Night, Frances E. Dolan
Romeo and Juliet, Catherine Belsey
King Lear, Jean Howard
A Midsummer Night's Dream, Heidi Brayman Hackel

Macbeth

Language and Writing

EMMA SMITH

B L O O M S B U R Y
LONDON • NEW DELHI • NEW YORK • SYDNEY

Bloomsbury Arden Shakespeare

An imprint of Bloomsbury Publishing Plc

50 Bedford Square	175 Fifth Avenue
London	New York
WC1B 3DP	NY 10010
UK	USA

www.bloomsbury.com

First published 2013

British Library Cataloguing-in-Publication Data
A catalogue record for this book is available from the British Library.

ISBN HB:	978-1-4725-1828-6
PB:	978-1-4081-5290-4
ePDF:	978-1-4725-0041-0
ePub:	978-1-4081-5603-2

Library of Congress Cataloging-in-Publication Data
A catalogue record for this book is available from the British Library.

Typeset by Newgen Imaging Systems Pvt Ltd, Chennai, India

CONTENTS

SERIES EDITOR'S PREFACE

This series puts the pedagogical expertise of distinguished literary critics at the disposal of students embarking upon Shakespeare Studies at university. While they demonstrate a variety of approaches to the plays, all the contributors to the series share a deep commitment to teaching and a wealth of knowledge about the culture and history of Shakespeare's England. The approach of each of the volumes is direct yet intellectually sophisticated and tackles the challenges Shakespeare presents. These volumes do not provide a short-cut to Shakespeare's works but instead offer a careful explication of them directed towards students' own processing and interpretation of the plays and poems.

Students' needs in relation to Shakespeare revolve overwhelmingly around language, and Shakespeare's language is what most distinguishes him from his rivals and collaborators – as well as what most embeds him in his own historical moment. The *Language and Writing* series understands language as the very heart of Shakespeare's literary achievement rather than as an obstacle to be circumvented. This series addresses the difficulties often encountered in reading Shakespeare alongside the necessity of writing papers for university examinations and course assessment. The primary objective here is to foster rigorous critical engagement with the texts by helping students develop their own critical writing skills. *Language and Writing* titles demonstrate how to develop students' own capacity to articulate and enlarge upon their experience of encountering the text, far beyond summarizing, paraphrasing or 'translating' Shakespeare's language into a more palatable, contemporary form. Each of the volumes in the series introduces the text as an act of specifically literary language and shows that the multifarious issues of life and history that Shakespeare's work addresses cannot be separated from their expression in language. In addition, each book takes students through a series of guidelines about how to develop viable undergraduate critical essays on the text in question, not by delivering interpretations, but rather by taking readers step-by-step through the process of discovering and developing their own critical ideas.

All the books include chapters examining the text from the point of view of its composition, that is, from the perspective of Shakespeare's own process of composition as a reader, thinker and writer. The opening chapters consider when and how the play was written, addressing, for example, the extant literary and cultural acts of language, from which Shakespeare constructed his work – including his sources – as well as the generic, literary and theatrical conventions at his disposal. Subsequent sections demonstrate how to engage in detailed examination and analysis of the text and focus on the literary, technical and historical intricacies of Shakespeare's verse and prose. Each volume also includes some discussion of performance. Other chapters cover textual issues as well as the interpretation of the extant texts for any given play on stage and screen, treating for example, the use of stage directions or parts of the play that are typically cut in performance. Authors also address issues of stage/film history as they relate to the cultural evolution of Shakespeare's words. In addition, these chapters deal with the critical reception of the work, particularly the newer theoretical and historicist approaches that have revolutionized our understanding of Shakespeare's language over the past 40 years. Crucially, every chapter contains a section on 'Writing matters', which links the analysis of Shakespeare's language with students' own critical writing.

The series empowers students to read and write about Shakespeare with scholarly confidence and hopes to inspire their enthusiasm for doing so. The authors in this series have been selected because they combine scholarly distinction with outstanding teaching skills. Each book exposes the reader to an eminent scholar's teaching in action and expresses a vocational commitment to making Shakespeare accessible to a new generation of student readers.

Professor Dympna Callaghan
Series Editor
Arden Student Skills: Language and Writing

PREFACE

Macbeth's downfall is his inability to read.

This might seem an excessive claim: misreading is, after all, a long way down this serial murderer's charge list. But Macbeth's misinterpretation of the witches' prophecies is fatal. In believing he can translate their speech from the riddlingly exact 'none of woman born/ Shall harm Macbeth' (4.1.80–1) into the more prosaic 'I'm invincible', Macbeth adds a tin-eared inattention to linguistic precision to his more manifest failings. Nuance and specificity escape him, just as compassion does. The witches' language is literally untranslatable: its form and its content are intertwined, 'in a double sense' (5.8.20). Macbeth commits the heresy of paraphrase, and in doing so, is engaged in the same involvement with language as are we readers. The phrase 'heresy of paraphrase' comes from an influential literary critical manifesto that argues exactly against paraphrase as a critical tool, because 'the paraphrase is not the real core of meaning which constitutes the essence of the poem' (Brooks, 180). In this way, the witches are poets, and Macbeth is a reader who, rather as we will do during the course of this book, comes to recognize the intrinsic ambiguity of the text in front of him. He sees that they 'palter' (5.8.20) with him – a word meaning to trick with words, or to prevaricate, or equivocate (another resonant word in the play). This paltering, however, is intrinsic to Shakespeare's own finely calibrated language and construction, in which doubleness and a shifting gap between words and their referents function to structure the play's terrifying exploration of ambition and agency.

In focusing on the language of the play, this guide aims to develop your appreciation and enjoyment of this dense, psychological thriller. Unlike other guides to the play aimed at students or playgoers, however, this one does not promise 'no fear Shakespeare' or 'Shakespeare made easy' or 'Shakespeare made simple'. As one recent book puts it, *Shakespeare is Hard, But So is Life;* or, to put it another way, Shakespeare's language has to conjure and give shape to intense emotion and action in the play, and it does so by mirroring that passion in its texture and its invention. Macbeth comes to learn that 'Macbeth shall never vanquish'd be, until/ Great Birnam wood to high Dunsinane hill/ Shall come against him' (4.1.92–4) does *not* mean 'Macbeth will not be beaten.' Similarly, this book will show that Shakespeare's words cannot properly be translated or paraphrased, but also that they *need* not be. The historian of language David Crystal encourages us: 'All fluent modern English speakers, native or non-native, have an immensely powerful start, in that they already know over 90 per cent of the language that Shakespeare uses' (Crystal, 15).

As Shakespeare's shortest tragedy *Macbeth* has an intensity and pace of language and plot that is unique in the canon. Writing of the modernist novelist James Joyce, Samuel Beckett observed that 'His writing is not about something. It is that something itself' (Beckett, 14). Beckett denies the referentiality we usually expect from writing – that it is *about* something, or has a meaning outside of itself – and instates instead a pleasure in the aesthetic texture of the language itself: in *Macbeth*, too, language is 'the thing itself', and enhancing the enjoyment and appreciation of that thing is the aim of this study.

Everything in the play – character, theme, setting, plot – is language, from its moral and physical darkness to its creation of its protagonist's guilty mind, and repeatedly, linguistic effects turn out to perform the play's larger ethical and dramatic manoeuvres. In Perthshire in Scotland you can visit the 'The Macbeth Experience', which promises 'a multi-media presentation' bringing the 'historical facts'; about the warrior king, plus 'extensive gift shop and restaurant'. But the real *Macbeth* experience, this book will argue, is a linguistic one.

Like Shakespeare, we don't need to go to Scotland. The play
has nothing to do with historical facts – remember, the writing
is 'not about something'. Rather, it renders dramatic action in
intensely interior and verbal ways.

This book

This book is divided into five major sections, with subhead-
ings to help direct the reader to parts of specific interest. But it
stresses the interconnectedness of language, theme, plot, and
character, and some aspects come up more than once.

The Introduction establishes the play's position in
Shakespeare's writing career, not only among the tragedies but also in an arc of plays concerned with deposition
and regicide, from *Richard III* through *Julius Caesar* and
Hamlet to *Macbeth*. This chronology allows us to situate
Shakespeare's increasing and ambivalent sympathy for the
'villain' in these dramas of ambition and power, which
reaches its high point in *Macbeth*. The play will be considered in the Jacobean context, as a play which responds to
the Scottish King James' reign in England, but perhaps not
in the entirely ingratiating way that critics have sometimes
asserted. In a brief overview of criticism we get some bear-
ings on the different ways in which readers have engaged, and
students can and will engage, with the play's language. This
book, though, is not a critical survey – very good versions
of that kind of book already exist (see Further Reading). Its
emphasis is on your own reading and your confidence with
Shakespeare's language.

Chapter One begins with an apparently obvious question: 'What is *Macbeth*?' Are we all reading the same
thing? We will discuss the printing history of the play and
the ways in which modern texts take editorial decisions to
make the play more accessible to us, but in doing so, may
smooth out some meaningful aspects of the play as it was
first published in 1623. We then go on to consider language

at the micro-level: the way in which words build into lines and speeches, through an analysis of Macbeth's soliloquy at the beginning of 1.7. The chapter then opens out, building these individual words into a more thoroughgoing thematic analysis of the role of domestic vocabulary in the tragedy, drawing out why critics have felt troubled by the play's variety of linguistic tone, and what this might tell us about the plot and its characters. The scene of Banquo's ghost (3.4) is a particular focus for this thematic discussion. The writing matters section encourages you to use the techniques outlined, including the use of online facsimiles of the First Folio text, searching through electronic concordances, thinking as theatrical voice coaches and literary practical critics do, in order not to explain or simplify Shakespeare's language but to understand and appreciate it.

Chapter Two focuses on a different unit of sense in the play: the way language builds the play's structure. We use a variety of tools to understand the way the play is built, and the way in which linguistic variation and echo help to unify its dramatic architecture. Thinking about the play as a suspense narrative akin to modern horror films helps us to see the underlying skeleton – as it were – of the structure of *Macbeth*. We also look extensively at what Shakespeare has done with his source material, Holinshed's compendious history book or *Chronicles*, at certain crucial points including the first meeting of Macbeth and Banquo with the Weird Sisters and the conversation between Malcolm and Macduff in England. In writing matters you can develop the insights gained from comparing Shakespeare's writing with its sources, and think further about the way modern film versions of the play bring out or redefine aspects of its structure.

In Chapter Three the emphasis is on language and character. We begin by looking at how the popular 'curse of *Macbeth*', which means the name of the play should not be spoken in a theatre for fear of terrible bad luck, connects unexpectedly to the play's own interest in the power, and danger, of the spoken word. This raises questions of agency in the play: is this play directed by supernatural, or human, forces? We investigate the way character is constructed linguistically, first by thinking about the cue-scripts from which early modern actors understood their roles and then turning to modern voice coaches, including Cicely Berry and Patsy Rodenburg, both adept at working with actors who are trying to get to grips with Shakespeare's language. The second half of the chapter considers some of the ways in which the language of the play erases, as well as constructs, individual character, and we finish by thinking about one of the most famous, and much mocked, questions in Shakespearean criticism: 'How many children had Lady Macbeth?'

Chapter Four reviews much of what has already been discussed by gathering material in response to different questions about the play. I have taken questions from college syllabi and online message boards to get a sense of the kind of writing assignments students are set. Some of them invite naive answers, but by putting forward Shakespeare's language, rather than, say, plot or character, as our primary evidential basis, we will be able to recuperate and redirect inadequate questions into sophisticated responses. This is not a section of ideal answers – far from it – but a series of suggestions of the kind of linguistic arguments that might be brought to bear in response to different questions.

Introduction

Macbeth in Shakespeare's career

Shakespeare began his work as an actor and playwright in London at the end of the 1580s or early 1590s. During the first decade he concentrated mostly on romantic comedies and on plays based on English history; around the turn of the seventeenth century, he turns towards tragedy and thence to a group of comedies at the end of his career sometimes called romances. *Macbeth* comes from the last quarter of Shakespeare's writing career. He probably wrote it in 1606 (see below for the particular echoes of contemporary events in the play). In chronological terms it comes amid other tragedies including *King Lear* and *Anthony and Cleopatra*, after *Hamlet* and *Othello* and before *Coriolanus*, the last of Shakespeare's tragedies before he moves to the romances.

It shares a good deal with these other plays in the tragic genre: its use of soliloquy, its suspicion of women's agency, its interrogation of the resonant idea of 'nothing' and its depiction of interiority. *Macbeth*, though, extends Shakespeare's manipulation of the tragic genre in its unflinching depiction of a murderer. The judgement on Shakespeare's other tragic characters is often debatable, as their plays depict them as foolish or wronged, 'more sinned against than sinning' (King Lear's depiction of himself at 3.2.60), 'one that loved not wisely, but too well' (Othello's final self-summary at 5.2.344). Such ethical ameliorations of Macbeth's deeds are not permitted. The comic writer James Thurber's 'The Macbeth Murder Mystery' presents an avid detective-fiction reader encountering the play and pronouncing that Macbeth 'didn't do it' (according to the rules of the detective genre, the most obvious murderer is, of course, never the real criminal). The reason this is funny is that it layers doubt onto a play which actually has very little of it. We see the Macbeths plan the murder and cover their traces afterwards. 'It may be', suggests Janette Dillon, 'that Shakespeare wrote the play precisely in order to test the limits of tragedy with this question: "can a monster be a tragic hero?"' (Dillon, 124). But he also seems to have written it to try to understand a 'monster' from within. For much of *Macbeth* we are caught inside the murderer's world and made to share his crazy, haunted perspective, as when, for instance, we see the ghost of Banquo when none of the guests does. And this empathy is achieved largely through a dynamic use of the device of soliloquy (speaking alone on stage): a dramatic technique that, for Shakespeare, seems to indicate that in its speaker there is a fascinating but potentially dangerous gap between his external appearance and inner emotion. In *Macbeth* he develops that insight in its most compelling way: Macbeth himself lacks the artfulness that often structures Hamlet's cleverly philosophical analyses of his situation, and tends to think within, rather than about, his situation. Macbeth's soliloquies capture the present-tense sense of his nervy, guilt-ridden existence.

In his earlier tragedies, Shakespeare might be said to be concerned with the causes of particular actions. For Hamlet, finding out the cause of his father's death structures the play towards a final conclusion; Iago works on Othello's insecurity to bring about the murder of Desdemona in the play's final act. But here in *Macbeth*, as in *King Lear*, the focus is more on consequences than causes. Here, the decisive action happens early in the play, and the subsequent scenes show how its effects ripple through the playworld. What happens to Macbeth after the murder of Duncan is of more interest in this play than the question of why Macbeth murders Duncan. This distinction changes the structure of the tragedy. Where other tragedies end with a bloodbath – the deaths of the Danish royal family at the end of *Hamlet*, for instance, or the 'tragic loading' of the corpse-strewn bed at the end of *Othello* (5.2.363) – in *Macbeth* blood is a central theme throughout. The apparently circumstantial question which opens the play's second scene, 'what bloody man is that?' (1.2.1) serves as a kind of epigraph to the whole play. Like its hero, the play of *Macbeth* is, within a short, intense spell, 'in blood/ Stepp'd in so far, that [. . .] Returning were as tedious as go o'er' (3.4.135–7). The contemporary dramatist Thomas Heywood wrote of tragedy 'beginning in calms, and ending in tempest', but from the start, *Macbeth* is marked by the brutal violence of war and treachery and the cosmic disturbance of the witches.

If *Macbeth* shares certain features with Shakespeare's other tragedies, it also has some other important generic connections. Macbeth's allusion to 'Tarquin's ravishing strides' (2.1.55) recalls Shakespeare's early narrative poem *The Rape of Lucrece*, perhaps his earliest examination of the evil-doer meditating on the brink of his deed. Tarquin wrestles with his conscience: 'What win I if I gain the thing I seek?/A dream, a breath, a froth of fleeting joy./Who buys a minute's mirth to wail a week,/Or sells eternity to get a toy?' (211–14). In allying himself with Tarquin, Macbeth equates regicide with the kind of physical desecration enacted on Lucrece in the poem. There are other affiliations too. In an age preoccupied with monarchical succession and, in particular, the question of who would succeed the childless Elizabeth I on the English throne, Shakespeare wrote a series of plays discussing regicide and regime change, many of them based on English history. In *Richard III* (c. 1593), the central figure, Richard Duke of Gloucester, plots his way to the throne. His Machievellian performance right from the play's first lines creates the audience as accomplice to his machinations: he is a kind of Macbeth who is theatrical rather than inward, relishing his crimes rather than struggling with their psychological consequences.

In *Richard II* (1595) Shakespeare shows the sequence of events by which Richard is deposed by his royal cousin Henry Bolingbroke. The play's earliest editions nominate it a 'tragedy': Richard is the central figure in a tragic pattern common from medieval literature – the so-called de casibus or fall of princes genre. Richard's role in the play is utterly dominant: throughout, Bolingbroke is either absent or laconic, in sharp contrast to his eloquent and self-dramatizing antagonist. The focus here is on deposition from the point of view of the reigning king – the equivalent, if you like, of the story of Macbeth told with the focus on Duncan.

Shakespeare's next regicide play is in a different context: the Roman history of *Julius Caesar* (1599), where it is in part Caesar's ambition to become king and end the republic that prompts Cassius and Brutus to kill him. Caesar's death is the central tableau of the play: stabbed by the conspirators in the Capitol, his corpse lies on stage for some 400 lines (the modern Shakespeare director Greg Doran tells us that performed Shakespeare goes at about 800 lines per hour, so this is a substantial period of stage-time), and the play explores the political and psychological consequences of his execution under the scrutiny of his watchful ghost. Again, the comparison with *Macbeth* is fruitful: *Julius Caesar* is a more explicitly political depiction of the transfer of power, and, while Brutus is isolated and has something of the tragic hero about him, the assassination is a collective act by the conspirators. Emrys Jones discusses these influences: 'what [Macbeth] "does" is comparable to what Richard [III] "does"; what he "is" is more like what Brutus "is" (and, we may add, Tarquin)' (Jones, 205).

Stories of deposition continued to attract Shakespeare, including the ousted dukes of *As You Like It* and *The Tempest*. In *Hamlet* (c. 1600) the representation of regicide is recalled, not staged, just as Polonius recalls playing Caesar in a theatrical in-joke connecting the play to the previous *Julius Caesar*: here the murdered king Old Hamlet cries for revenge from his son, while his killer, Claudius, is allowed only glimpses of regret and humanity in a play dominated by the central ego of Prince Hamlet. In effect this gives us *Macbeth* told from the point of view of Malcolm.

The structure of *Macbeth* grows out of and inverts these precedents. In placing the murder of king Duncan in Act 2, less than a quarter of the way through the play, the balance of interest is decisively tipped towards Macbeth. This is a tragedy of regicide told from the point of view of usurper (Richard III, Bolingbroke, Brutus, Claudius) not victim (Richard II, Caesar, Old Hamlet). But it is also a kind of revenge tragedy, in which it is the criminal, not the revenger, who is the focus. Like earlier plays in this popular Elizabethan genre, including Shakespeare's own *Hamlet*, *Macbeth* depicts a series of murders for which the law cannot give redress, since the king himself is their perpetrator. Thus they can only be avenged extra-judicially. The killing of a king and the disinheriting of his heir is a recognized cue for a revenge play. Macbeth, however, is far more than the conventional villain of the genre, and Malcolm, who ought to be in the role of revenging son, is far less than that dramatic prototype: their relative structural and ethical importance is reversed. In *Hamlet* revenge plots are multiplied: Hamlet has to take revenge for his father's death, but in killing Polonius he becomes the revenge object for another son, Laertes; meanwhile, the Norwegian prince Fortinbras is taking cold revenge for lands lost by his father. Similarly, the conclusion of *Macbeth* divides the political and familial revenges: Macduff kills Macbeth in revenge for his own family; Malcolm succeeds to the throne in a kind of political recompense for the murder of his father.

In *Julius Caesar* Shakespeare began an investigation into the mind of a political assassin. Brutus is a man who has no personal quarrel with the emperor, but believes Caesar's ambition to be dangerous to the state of Rome. Brutus knows that he puts his own peace into jeopardy when he joins the conspiracy against his leader. Insomniac and pondering the crime – an anticipation of Macbeth – he articulates the terrible wait between thought and deed: 'Between the acting of a dreadful thing/ And the first motion, all the interim is / Like a phantasma or a hideous dream' (2.1.63–5). In *Hamlet* Shakespeare gave, momentarily, a snapshot of Claudius's unquiet mind in his thwarted prayer 'my offence is rank, it smells to heaven' (3.3.36). In *Macbeth* these hints are amplified into a thorough interrogation of the mind of the murderer: the play's queasy achievement is to provoke that 'sympathy by which we enter into his feelings and are made to understand them', as Thomas de Quincey put it (De Quincey, 91). 'In the early scenes we are probably on more intimate terms with Macbeth than we are with any other of Shakespeare's characters' (Jones, 195). Shakespeare's achievement in *Macbeth* is to bring us into this sympathy, this intimacy, with its violent, vulnerable anti-hero and to balance our empathy and judgement. When Malcolm proclaims himself king he dismisses 'the dead butcher, and his fiend-like Queen' (5.9.35): the description echoes with its brutal inadequacy to the complex persons we have seen on stage.

Macbeth in historical context

The year 1606 was a turbulent one in early modern England. Three years previously James VI of Scotland had succeeded Elizabeth I on the English throne. One of his first actions was to take up the patronage of Shakespeare's acting company, who became the King's Men. As chief dramatist of the King's Men, Shakespeare turned his drama towards royal interests. Many plays of the early seventeenth century engage with political themes close to James – the issue of the division of the kingdoms in *King Lear*, for instance, addresses his ambition to unify his kingdoms of England and Scotland with reference to the ancient kingdom of Britain – but nowhere is this more sustained than in *Macbeth*. Not only does the play take up Scottish themes, but it also engages with James' own claim to be descended from the historical Banquo. In the process it exonerates from blame the character inherited from the chronicle sources, which state that Banquo was privy to the murder of Duncan: 'communicating his purposed intent with his trusty friends, amongst whom Banquo was the chiefest, upon confidence of their promised aid, [Macbeth] slew the king at Enverns' (see Chapter Two for more on Shakespeare's use of Holinshed). It is often suggested that the witches' final conjuration to Macbeth, that 'show of eight kings, the last with a glass in his hand: Banquo following' (4.1.111SD), would have held up a mirror to reflect James' own place in the genealogy of Scottish futurity in an early performance at court. Furthermore, although Shakespeare had touched on themes of witchcraft in his earlier history plays, especially in the characters of Joan la Pucelle and Margaret of Anjou in *1* and *2 Henry VI*, this play's specific foregrounding of the Weird Sisters directly speaks to James' own attested fascination with the supernatural and with magic. Before coming to the English throne he had written a book on the topic, *Daemonologie* (1597), and he continued an active and evolving interest in contemporary debates between empirical and supernatural explanations for witchcraft.

But the truism that Shakespeare wrote the play to ingratiate himself with the monarch has undergone some important modification by recent critics who have pointed out that there is no evidence it was ever performed before King James (and relatively little opportunity for it to have been so), and, further, that the character of Banquo is not quite so whitewashed as his royal descendant might have wished (Barroll). What are those 'cursed thoughts' (2.1.8) he admits, and why can he not sleep – the play's ultimate signal of a guilty conscience? If Shakespeare had intended a complete ethical makeover for the equivocal historical figure of Banquo for James' benefit, he might have done a more thorough job of it. Perhaps, as has been suggested, the play addressed its depiction of regal tyranny to the increasingly absolutist James in a more satiric or subversive spirit, marking his unpopularity rather than toadying to his wishes. If contemporary references to the play are an index of its popularity, then *Macbeth* seems to have been markedly less favoured than Shakespeare's other tragedies: maybe this suggests it was not a success.

Macbeth is a play of its period in more direct ways, too. In November 1605, a Catholic plot to blow up the king and his Parliament was discovered in a Westminster cellar. The Gunpowder Plot, including the conspirator Guy Fawkes, has entered English folklore, with bonfires, fireworks and the burning of effigies still called 'guys' on 5 November every year. Because of its connections with his native Stratford-upon-Avon (the conspirators had met at Clopton Hall just outside the town, and many of them were from Warwickshire), Shakespeare may have been particularly interested in the details of the plot, but it is hard to think that there was anyone in London in 1606 who was not preoccupied by this breach of homeland security. In the resulting atmosphere of feverish excitement and the show-trials of the conspirators in the early weeks of 1606, a number of linguistic terms came to epitomize the plot, particularly the word 'blow', a crucial term in the letter that revealed the plot, and one which James correctly interpreted as a reference to an explosion. In addition the word 'equivocate', a term, like 'palter', associated with the language of political and ethical evasion and its Jesuit manipulators, emerged as a keynote of the news coverage of the post-plot period. 'Blow' is used by Macbeth to refer to the proposed murder (1.7.4). 'Equivocate' emerges six times in *Macbeth*, all but one in the scene with the Dunsinane porter responding to the knocking of Ross and Macduff (2.3). A production by the Royal Shakespeare Company in 2011 directed by Michael Boyd updated the play's intrinsic connections to terrorist violence by having the laughing porter menacingly reveal sticks of dynamite hidden in his coat, in a disturbing conflation of cartoon iconography and modern suicide bomber.

There are other echoes too: in a speech to Parliament days after the thwarted plot, James recalled previous attempts on his life in symbolic terms that reverberate with the play's own curious imagery of daggers and bloody children (see Chapter Three). These highly charged words, and the atmosphere of suspicion and terror suffusing *Macbeth*, resonate with the political climate in which the play was conceived and performed. But Shakespeare is not a propagandist writer or an apologist for official policies. If we compare *Macbeth* to a more explicit reaction to the Gunpowder Plot, Thomas Dekker's play *The Whore of Babylon* (1607) with its lampoon of the Catholic hierarchy and binary juxtaposition of the wicked Babylonian empress with the virtuous 'Titania', or Queen Elizabeth, we can see an immediate difference. *Macbeth* is less about a simplistic identification of Catholicism as the enemy and more about the effects of fear, terror and guilt on a population and an individual. If it is not directly 'about' the Gunpowder Plot in any obvious way, then, *Macbeth* is marked by its legacy of political and social unease.

Although there are some traces of a Macbeth story in the records before the Jacobean period, most critics date the play to the months immediately following the trial of the Gunpowder Plot conspirators in 1606 (although if we allow the possibility of revision, as discussed in Chapter One, the dating becomes multiple and more uncertain). A ship called the *Tiger* returned to England in June 1606 after a difficult voyage that by some calculations lasted, possibly coincidentally, 'seven nights nine times nine' (or 567 days, $7 \times 9 \times 9$), and this may therefore have inspired the First Witch's plans in 1.3. As Chapter One discusses, the text as first printed in 1623 may be different from that written and performed early in the Jacobean period.

Macbeth in criticism

The earliest interpretations of *Macbeth*, as for most Shakespeare plays, are rewritings. William Davenant's stage adaptation was first performed when the theatres reopened at the restoration of Charles II. It was largely rewritten, particularly to make the language more comprehensible and less densely poetic. It expanded the role of the witches into a spectacular musical and visual component (the play was praised by Samuel Pepys for its 'variety of dancing and music' (Brooke, 37)), and added to Lady Macduff's role so that she became a virtuous opposite of Lady Macbeth's vice. In the eighteenth century, the scholar-editors' view of *Macbeth* tended to stress its 'grandeur': Samuel Johnson felt it 'has no nice discrimina-tions of character', but that 'the passions are directed to their true end. Lady Macbeth is merely detested; and though the courage of Macbeth preserves some esteem yet every reader rejoices at his fall'. Johnson, and the neo-classical taste which he represents, felt the witches were more appropriate to 'fairy tales instead of tragedies' (Johnson, 51; 62).

Character-based approaches to the play began at the end of the eighteenth century and were to dominate the next cen-tury and a half. William Hazlitt's *Characters of Shakespeare's Plays* (1817) drew on the author's theatre-going as well as his literary appreciation. His descriptions are compelling: 'Macbeth himself appears driven along by the violence of his fate like a vessel drifting before a storm: he reels to and fro like a drunken man'; Lady Macbeth 'we fear more than we hate'; the witches he deems 'ridiculous on the modern stage'. Hazlitt emphasizes a 'systematic principle of contrast' in the play he judges as a 'constant struggle between life and death' (Bate, 423–7). The poet Samuel Taylor Coleridge stressed the theme of speed in the play, and focused interestingly on the character of Lady Macbeth, who he judged bore 'the mock fortitude of a mind deluded by ambition' (Bate, 418). Anna Jameson, who wrote on Shakespeare's female characters, argued that Lady Macbeth should not 'be cast beyond the pale of our sympa-thies' (Bate, 441). Jameson admired her 'amazing power of intellect', even as she had to recognize that she is 'as fearful in herself as her deeds are hateful' (Bate, 441). Perhaps the most influential Romantic essay on *Macbeth* was by the writer Thomas De Quincey. His 'On the Knocking at the Gate in *Macbeth*' described the murder of Duncan as a kind of trance, 'locked up and sequestered in some deep recess' from which the knocking at the castle gate in 2.2–2.3 wakes the play: 'the human has made its reflux upon the fiendish; the pulses of life are beginning to beat again' (De Quincey, 93).

Twentieth-century criticism of the play developed the inter-est in the language and in the characters. A. C. Bradley's

Shakespearean Tragedy stressed character as the driving force in tragedy: 'the calamities and catastrophe follow inevitably from the deeds of men, and . . . the main source of these deeds is character' (Bradley, 7), and he developed his readings of Macbeth and Lady Macbeth accordingly. By treating the characters as patients in his 'Some Character-Types Met with in Psycho-Analytical Work' (1916), Sigmund Freud develops Bradley's approach, stressing the importance of childlessness to the couple. As Chapter Three will discuss, Bradley's stress on character was countered by the New Critics' emphasis on poetic imagery. Caroline Spurgeon identified four major image clusters in the play: clothing, sound and space, darkness and light, and sin as disease. Cleanth Brooks developed a detailed analysis of the pattern of imagery associated with the 'naked babe', linking it to the image of the clothed man in the play. These critical approaches of the first half of the twentieth century thus stressed the aesthetic and psychological aspects of the play, broadly subscribing to a view of the tragedy that saw violence as the aberrant disruption of a natural harmony which is restored in the final scenes.

Later-twentieth-century readings of the play tended to stress its brutality as political rather than poetic. Jan Kott, a Polish theatre director whose book translated as *Shakespeare Our Contemporary* has been highly influential, stresses its uncomfortable proximity to 'the Auschwitz experience': 'there is only one theme in *Macbeth*: murder' (Kott, 69). In his article on the opening scenes of the play, Harry Berger echoed this, stressing the ways the play is built on violence from the very outset, rather than, as criticism had tended to assert, that the murder of Duncan changes everything. A more morally uncertain play emerges. This more ambiguous tragedy has preoccupied recent critics. Feminist readings by Coppélia Kahn and Janet Adelman have stressed the importance of, and anxieties about feminine power in the play. The witches have been the subject of provocative studies. Terry Eagleton argues that in their ambiguous appearance and riddling speech they challenge hierarchical order and are thus the heroines of the play. Diane Purkiss emphasizes the theatricality of the witches and argues that their purpose is really sensationalist rather than political or philosophical. Stephen Orgel identifies the witches with rebellious female power. Malcolm Evans took the title of his deconstructive book *Signifying Nothing* from the play: his analysis of *Macbeth* stresses the intrinsic equivocality of the play's language not as poetic ambiguity but political subversion.

Recent criticism has returned to the issue of the play's original topicality. Gary Wills' *Witches and Jesuits: Shakespeare's Macbeth* gives a detailed exploration of the impact of the Gunpowder Plot on the play. Leeds Barroll is sceptical about claims the play was written to please King James, pointing out the paucity of evidence. Accounts of the play in performance on stage and screen by John Wilders and Bernice Kliman, as well as insights from actors such as Derek Jacobi, Sinead Cusack and Harriet Walter, exemplify the ways in which performance is at the centre of contemporary Shakespeare studies. Finally, the question of Middleton's involvement in the playtext is fully explored in the recent *Thomas Middleton: The Collected Works* where the text printed uses typographical differentiation to separate out the proposed contributions of the two authors.

CHAPTER ONE

Language: Words, lines, speeches

In this chapter we will draw out some skills of close analysis for use in the analysis of Shakespeare's dramatic poetry, using Macbeth's soliloquy in 1.7 as a particular focus. First, the nature of the text and issues of editing the play are discussed, before thinking about the vocabulary, rhythms and intrinsic knottiness of Macbeth's first long speech.

What is *Macbeth*?

All instructions on how to study Shakespeare, or indeed any poetic literature, will stress that your interpretations must not be based on conjecture or assertion, but on close quotation from the text itself. The Writing Center at Harvard University advises students to begin with the 'close reading of a text', and proposes three stages of study: (1) read with a pencil in hand to annotate the text (this was probably how Renaissance readers read, too, although the lead pencil as we know it was a slightly later invention); (2) look for patterns in things you've noticed about the text; (3) ask questions about the patterns you've noticed. It's a good sequence, but it is clear that it begins with a presupposition: the text. The idea of the text here is a stable one: we all know what it is, and it pre-exists our reading of it. This common-sense assertion is questioned by lots of different literary theories, especially reader–response criticism, which argues that the text only really comes into being when it is read: it's a literary version of that philosophical thought experiment 'if a tree falls in a forest and no-one hears it fall, does it make any sound?'

Aside from the more theoretical questions about the relation between the text and the reader, in the case of Shakespeare's plays there are also practical questions. Just what is the 'text' on which we must perform this close reading? Is the text of a play the words on the page, or is that merely a secondary product, a script capturing only one element of a three-dimensional, multi-sensory performance? Early modern plays were performances first, and only secondarily, and then only sometimes, books. Sometimes scholars talk about how we can imagine the plays in the theatre as a movement from 'page to stage': in fact the rhyme needs to be reversed, since the process was of imagining early modern plays in book form, from 'stage to page'. This study will bring in performances – historical, contemporary, imaginary – to corroborate and to question some of its more literary close readings. But let us begin with some details of how the play in front of us came to be there. What is the 'text' of *Macbeth*?

Macbeth in print: the 1623 Folio

Although *Macbeth* was probably performed in 1606 and revived in 1610, it was not published until the posthumous collected edition of Shakespeare's plays known as the First Folio was printed in 1623. This book, containing 36 plays (*Pericles* and *The Two Noble Kinsmen*, both collaborative plays, are not included, and nor are the poems *Venus and Adonis* and *The Rape of Lucrece* or the sonnets), was prepared for publication by two of Shakespeare's fellow actors, John Heminges and Henry Condell. Its long title *Mr William*

Shakespeares Comedies, Histories, & Tragedies. Published according to the True Originall Copies indicates its principle of organization: by genre. *Macbeth* appears in the tragedies, between *Julius Caesar* and *Hamlet*.

No manuscript copies of Shakespeare's plays exist, except for a few contested pages of Shakespeare's probable contribution to a collaborative and unperformed play, *Thomas More*. All our editions, therefore, derive from printed texts, and all printed texts are marked by hands other than the author's. In the case of drama, this includes performance-related changes made by the theatre company, perhaps at different times, as well as interventions by printers and others. We cannot know with certainty what Shakespeare himself wrote – nor how to take account of his own first and second thoughts, or the collective work of the theatre company in shaping the plays for performance. Even if we could disaggregate these roles, would that help us to produce a single text? Editors of other authors have always argued whether the author's first draft should have priority over their own later revision (such as in the case of Mary Shelley's *Frankenstein* or Wordsworth's *The Prelude*), and editors of drama always need to acknowledge the contributory role of the performance process – actors, directors, rehearsals – as well as the author in producing the text (after all, an unperformable stage play can hardly be the ideal version). Many modern plays, including Arthur Miller's *The Crucible*, Samuel Beckett's *Waiting for Godot* and Tony Kushner's *Angels in America* exist in different printed versions precisely because their texts record different moments in the dynamic life of the play moving from pen to stage and back again.

All we can know for sure about the text of *Macbeth*, therefore, is what was published in 1623. Whereas for other plays – *Hamlet* and *King Lear* are notable examples – editors have to tussle with two or even three early extant texts with equal claims to authority, *Macbeth* exists in a single text. It is generally assumed that the underlying text from which the printers worked was a theatre prompt-book (evidence for this includes the directions for offstage noises and the relatively complete entry and exit stage directions, which suggest a text prepared for use in the theatre).

Printing the Folio

Printing the thousand or so pages of the First Folio was a substantial logistical task, which took a consortium of publishers and more than a year to complete. The word Folio refers to a size: it indicates a book that has its pages made from a sheet of paper folded once – so that there are four pages of text, two on each side, to each sheet of paper. In the early modern period, this Folio format tended to bestow a weight – metaphorical as well as literal – on its contents, and was preferred for serious works such as bibles, atlases and histories: it was rare to see vernacular (English-language) plays in this prestigious product. Before Shakespeare only Ben Jonson had printed his plays, along with courtly entertainments and some poetry, in a Folio volume called *Works* (1616).

Letterpress printing involved the division of a manuscript into sections that would fit in a specific number of printed pages – a skilled process of estimation known as 'casting off' – because books were not typeset in sequence from beginning to end; rather, each printed sheet carried two pages which were not consecutive (look at the collate or booklet feature on a modern photocopier to get a sense of this). The printer would then set letters and punctuation marks as individual pieces of type in a framework called a 'forme', which was inked and placed on to the press so that the pages could be printed. Each page had a 'catchword' – the first word of the next page printed at the foot of the previous one – and a signature, a kind of page number, to enable the printed sheets to be assembled in the correct order. Books were sold unbound, as a stack of loose-leaf 'quires' or gatherings of printed paper. It is estimated that an unbound copy of the First Folio cost around one pound (for comparison, entrance to the theatre cost one penny, and the theatre's takings for a single perform-ance might be about three pounds).

Printers worked rapidly and were prone – though not as much as we might think – to errors. One of the compositors of the First Folio, known as Compositor E, made a large number of errors, which has led scholars to identify him with the inex-perienced John Leason, a new apprentice in Jaggard's print-ing shop who was only signed up a few months before the work on the Shakespeare volume. Such errors were not always picked up by proof-readers, who in any case looked out for obvious mistakes, like turned letters, rather than checking the printed text against the copy. Thus in *Macbeth* the error 'Soris' for 'Forres' at 1.3.39 was not noticed: as an unfa-miliar place–name the error does not stand out. Sometimes formes were corrected during the printing process – known as stop-press correction – but any sheets of the uncorrected text would still be used, since paper was too expensive to waste. About 15 per cent of the entire First Folio sheets have been corrected. Most extant copies of the First Folio are unique, in that their proportion of corrected/uncorrected sheets var-ies. In *Macbeth*, for instance, a mistaken Roffe (presumably an error misreading the long 's' format) was corrected to Rosse, and a stray 'my' deleted from the jumbled 'on my with' (4.3.154), but one editor calculates that more than 20 obvious typographical errors were not picked up by the proof-reading process. (Muir, xv), including 'Bartlet' for 'martlet' (1.6.4) or 'gallowgrasses' for 'gallowglasses' (1.2.113).

Editing the Folio

Digital versions of the First Folio online mean it is easy to consult the play as it first appeared, and transcriptions of the Folio text mean it is also possible to search that first edition. Anyone seriously interested in the play will want to consult these resources (see Further Reading). But most of us will read and study the play via a modern edition, for which an editor has made certain kinds of interpretative decisions to make the play more intelligible for us. Many of these seem uncontroversial. Lopping the final 'e' off an otherwise familiar word such as 'againe' or 'seene', or changing the ending 'ie' to 'y' in 'verie' or 'monkie' merely registers changes in spelling over the past 400 years; spelling was not standardized in the Shakespearean period, and it is unlikely anyway that the Folio preserves much of Shakespeare's own preferred spellings. Punctuation marks seem to have been as much a reflection of the print-shop compositors' own preferences (we can identify that two distinct workers set the type for *Macbeth*: their names are lost but bibliographers call them Compositor A and Compositor B) as of any feature of the underlying copy. Modernizing the Renaissance convention of printing 'v' for 'u', or of the long 's' which looks rather like a letter 'f' in early texts, makes it easier on the eye for readers unused to that convention. These are all print-house conventions – sometimes called 'accidentals' to distinguish them from more significant, probably authorial 'substantive' elements.

The most active intervention into the text of *Macbeth* by editors tends to happen around lineation. A number of passages are printed in verse that is irregular: editors tend to standardize to make it look more like the iambic pentameter characteristic of Shakespeare.

Lady Macbeth's entrance in 2.2 is an example of this relineation. Here is how it appears in the Folio text.

That which hath made them drunk, hath made me bold:
What hath quench'd them, hath giuen me fire.
Hearke, peace: it was the Owle that shriek'd,
The fatall Bell-man, which giues the stern'st good-night.
He is about it, the Doores are open:
And the surfeted Groomes doe mock their charge
With Snores. I haue drugg'd their Possets,
That Death and Nature doe contend about them,
Whether they liue, or dye. (Folio)

In the Arden text, as in many others, it has been edited:

> That which hath made them drunk, hath made me bold:
> What hath quench'd them, hath given me
>   fire. – Hark! – Peace!
> It was the owl that shriek'd, the fatal bellman
> Which gives the stern'st good-night. He is about it.
> The doors are open; and the surfeited grooms
> Do mock their charge with snores: I have drugg'd their
>   possets,
> That Death and Nature to contend about them
> Whether they live, or die. (Muir, 2.2.1–8)

This editing gives regular pentameter (ten-syllable) lines, reducing the total from nine Folio lines to eight edited ones. We may think this is a neater, more Shakespearean rhythm – but we might also be able to justify a more broken delivery by Lady Macbeth at this point. Shorter lines might indicate excitement, short breath, edginess, distraction – all potential features of her character at this heightened point in the play. That's to say the editorial relineation tidies things up, but may erase something that the actor could use to characterize their performance at this point, all because of the assumption that regular line lengths were Shakespeare's intention. Something similar happens with Lennox's description of the 'rough night' (2.3.61), another speech delivered under some strain or excitement, which takes up ten broken lines in the Folio and only seven in most modern relineated editions (2.3.54–61). You might want to compare these speeches with Macbeth's in 3.2: 'We have scorch'd the snake, not killed it' (13–26). This speech is 16 lines in the Folio, of which only half are metrically complete. Does your edition relineate – and if you were an editor, would you choose to, and if so, how?

Regularizing and modernizing spellings is another feature of editing that may sacrifice some specific and meaningful aspects of the early text in favour of a neater or more

standardized version. Margreta de Grazia and Peter Stallybrass
have noted that the word describing the witches that modern
editors routinely spell as 'weird' appears in the Folio text as
'weyard' or 'weyward'. The modern spelling, 'weird', identifies the witches primarily with the fates (*OED*: 'the principle,
power or agency by which events are predetermined; fate, destiny') – but these instances in *Macbeth* are the *Oxford English
Dictionary*'s only examples of 'weyard' or 'weyward' as alternative spellings for 'weird'. An alternative emendation, 'way-
ward', might bring out instead the extent to which the witches
transgress social norms (*OED*: 'disposed to go counter to the
wishes or advice of others, or to what is reasonable; wrong-
headed, intractable; froward, perverse'). This brings out a set
of meanings that are more to do with authority and political
control than with the mystifications of fate. Another editorial
choice is whether to retain, as Arden does, the antique form
'murther' for 'murder', or whether the word should simply be
modernized.

We might also consider punctuation differences as part of
this assessment of editorial intervention into Shakespeare's
text. Probably most of the punctuation in the modern edition you are using is editorial: looking at one of the online
folios you can see what changes have been made. Linguists
distinguish between punctuation as a 'phonetic' element –
meaning as a guide to pronunciation – or a 'grammatical'
one – meaning making the text easier to read. It may well be
that Shakespeare himself was not responsible for the punctuation in the text: the one piece of dramatic writing we think
we have in Shakespeare's own handwriting, speeches in the
composite manuscript of *Thomas More*, has hardly any punctuation at all. The following speech is taken from the Folio,
and next to it is a modern edition:

I coniure you, by that which you Professe,
(How ere you come to know it) answer me:
Though you vntye the Windes, and let them fight
Against the Churches: Though the yesty Waues

Confound and swallow Nauigation vp:
Though bladed Corne be lodg'd, & Trees blown downe,
Though Castles topple on their Warders heads:
Though Pallaces, and Pyramids do slope
Their heads to their Foundations: Though the treasure
Of Natures Germaine, tumble altogether,
Euen till destruction sicken: Answer me
To what I aske you. (Folio)

I conjure you, by that which you profess,
Howe'er you come to know it, answer me:
Though you untie the winds, and let them fight
Against the churches; though the yesty waves
Confound and swallow navigation up;
Though bladed corn be lodg'd, and trees blown down,
Though castles topple on their warders' heads;
Though palaces and pyramids do slope
Their heads to their foundations; though the treasure
Of nature's germen tumble all together,
Even till destruction sicken: answer me
To what I ask you. (Brooke, 4.1.64–75)

The Arden punctuation is slightly different, with a semi-colon after 'blown down' and commas after 'palaces' and 'pyramids' and 'sicken', thus slowing down the line and retaining the pattern of repeated punctuation in the anaphoric 'though' clauses, but offering the more correct modern version of semi-colons. The Royal Shakespeare Company (RSC) edition has 'Howe'er you come to know it' separated by dashes as an equivalent of the Folio parentheses (brackets tend to be used in subordinate clauses in the Folio, but their usage is quite different in the hands of different compositors), which neither other editor takes notice of, but this gives the speech a choppy look on the page and may convey more agitation in the speaker. (Something similar happens to Lady Macbeth's sleep-walking speeches in modern editions, which lose the relative grammatical coherence they have in the Folio by being broken up with dashes.) It would be hard to say that one of these was right and the others wrong, or even that one was necessarily better than the others, but what is clear is that punctuation, and the interpretative choices it emphasizes, is largely a construction of modern editors. As such it can be challenged by reference to other editions or to the Folio text. Consulting different editions will almost always bring out different emphases through punctuation. The edition of the play printed as part of the *Thomas Middleton: The Collected Works* (for Middleton's role in the play, see below), 'removes all punctuation and all capitalization at the beginning of sentences or verse lines . . . This completely unpunctuated text lets readers decide for themselves how to interpret the words' (Middleton, 1170). It's a radical solution, but one worth experimenting with for yourself.

Behind the removal of all the punctuation advocated in the Middleton edition is the belief that the punctuation of the Folio is neither authorial nor even purposeful in origin; it is 'accidental', to use terms from the theory of editing. By contrast, some actors believe that the Folio punctuation is substantive, in that it contains particular clues, perhaps direct from Shakespeare himself who was an actor as well as a playwright with the King's Men, about how the lines should be delivered orally. Such a view argues that, for example, actors should follow the Folio's use of full stops and treat Folio semi-colons as indicators of the word 'and' and colons as 'and therefore' or 'because'. It suggests that the apparently random distribution of initial capital letters in the Folio, for instance, indicates words of particular significance that, if the actor stresses them, help the speech to make psychological or dramatic sense. The director Patrick Tucker, one of the advocates of this method, calls the capitalized words 'stepping-stones'. Looking at a facsimile Folio gives you the opportunity to test that premis, as here in the Porter's grumbling as he attends the castle gate in 3.1:

Here's a knocking indeede: if a man were Porter of Hell
Gate, hee should have been old turning the Key. Knock.
Knock, Knock, Knock. Who's there i'th'name of Belzebub?
Here's a Farmer, that hang'd himselfe on th'expectation of
Plentie. Come in time, have Napkins enow about you.

It makes a kind of sense to emphasize the words, mostly
nouns, that are capitalized here, and it's also been suggested
that the word 'Farmer' would have recalled the Jesuit priest
Father Henry Garnett, who used it as an alias. Garnett was
hanged in the aftermath of the Gunpowder Plot. One interesting comparison point is a version of *Macbeth* in a genre
which also routinely uses typographical emphasis to focus
readerly attention on particular words, the graphic novel.
The collaboratively produced *Macbeth: The Graphic Novel*
(Litchborough: Classical Comics, 2008) represents the opening of the Porter's speech 'Here's a knocking, indeed! If a man
were porter of **hell-gate**, he should have old turning the key.
Knock, knock, knock. **Who's there**, i'th'name of Beelzebub?
Here's a **Farmer**, that **hanged** himself on the **expectation of
plenty**: come in time; have **napkins** enough aboutyou.' There's
some, but not complete, overlap with the pattern of capitalization in the same Folio passage as quoted above.

But at other times the use of capital letters seems less easy
to rationalize in this way, as here in the exchange between
Banquo and Macbeth from 2.1:

BANQUO.   All's well.
I dreamt last Night of the three weyward Sisters:
To you they have shew'd some truth.

MACBETH. I thinke not of them:
Yet when we can entreat an houre to serve
We would spend it in some words upon that Businesse,
If you would graunt the time.

BANQUO. At your kind'st leysure.

> MACBETH. If you shall cleave to my consent,
> Whe 'tis, shall make Honor for you.

Night, Businesse and Honor do not seem to be the only words of note or emphasis in the conversation, although actors could choose to work with the Folio capitalization as guidance.

Other features of a modern edition that we would now expect are not present in the Folio text. There is, for example, no list of characters, or *dramatis personae:* these are added by editors (and does yours, like the Arden, continue the eighteenth-century tradition of listing male characters first and female ones below?). The naming of characters is standardized. Throughout the Folio text, Lady Macbeth is called only 'Lady' in her stage directions and speech prefixes, and sometimes 'Macbeths lady', which suggests a lack of autonomy unfamiliar to many readings of her character. It comes as a surprise to see that she is never called Lady Macbeth in the text. Nor is she, as some modern editors add, ever called Queen in the apparatus of the text. Lady Macduff is called 'Wife' and her child 'Son', emphasizing their generic and familial, rather than personal, roles: a modern edition is more likely to add specific names to personalize them. The witches are called simply by numbers: 1, 2 and 3. If the editor chooses to add to the speech prefixes 'witch', that results in a text much more conscious of this term than the Folio, where the word 'witch' appears only a handful of times.

Macbeth is unusual among the Folio plays in being divided into both acts and scenes, comparable to those in modern editions although rendered in Latin: 'Actus Secundus. Scena Prima.' The final scenes of the battle in Act 5 are not divided as they are by modern editors: continuous staging in the early modern theatre may have meant that breaks in the action were an unnecessary deceleration of the play's conclusion. Scene breaks in early modern playtexts seem to be understood as moments when the stage is completely empty for a moment. This does mean that there are different scene divisions in different editions: the Oxford and the RSC editions have 7 scenes in Act 5, like the Folio; the Arden edition has 9 scenes; the Norton edition has 11. Older editions tend to use Roman numerals for act and scene divisions: here we will use the format 2.1 where the first number is the act, the second the scene and the third, where included, indicates the line numbers.

Stage directions

Many editors assume that stage directions in the play are not authorial and that therefore they can be more easily changed and emended than the actual speeches (the editorial convention is to place any additional stage directions within square brackets, but not all editions do this). Thus the 1951 Arden text supplies locations for the scenes that are not present in the Folio ([*Dunsinane. A room in the Castle*]), but such specification is at odds with the loose, flexible staging of the Globe which had no substantial sets to distinguish between settings. Where it is important for us to register where a scene takes place, the dialogue makes sure we get the information. Macbeth promises to kill Macduff's 'wife, his babes' (4.1.152): when we meet in the next scene a woman complaining about being left in danger by her husband, 'To leave his wife, to leave his babes' (4.2.6), we are in no doubt that this is the Castle of Fife. Likewise, two mentions of 'England' in 4.3 make clear where the scene takes place.

Elsewhere, adding clarificatory stage directions is often uncontroversial, but sometimes shapes the text in substantial ways. The Folio stage direction just before Arden's 5.9 has 'Enter fighting, and Macbeth slaine', which seems to suggest that Macbeth's death happens on stage (Arden has 'Re-enter fighting, and Macbeth slain'). The RSC and Oxford texts see a problem: how does Macbeth's body get off the stage? (In the theatre it needn't: at least one modern production has tarred Malcolm's new regime with some of the brutality of the old by having Macbeth's body trampled underfoot on stage as his successor is crowned). The RSC and Oxford texts add 'Exit Macduff with Macbeth's body' to indicate the choreography of the play's concluding movement.

Stage directions in the Folio text tend, as elsewhere in Shakespeare's work, to be minimal, particularly when it comes to descriptions about how a certain action or line should be performed. 'Witches vanish', for instance, gives no indication how this might have been achieved (the Globe theatre did have smoke and trapdoors which might help facilitate an incorporeal exit). When the apparitions appear to Macbeth in 4.1, the stage direction 'descends' for each one may indicate that the original staging saw 'an armed head', 'a bloody child' and 'a child crowned, with a tree in his hand' as a series of tableaux raised from beneath the stage through the trapdoor and then lowered again. The relative sparsity of stage directions is striking to modern readers. This extract from the opening of a much later play, and one also much concerned with witchcraft, Arthur Miller's *The Crucible*, makes the contrast clear:

> TITUBA [*already taking a step backward*]: My Betty be hearty soon?
> PARRIS: Out of here!
> TITUBA [*backing to the door*]: My Betty not goin' die . . .
> PARRIS [*scrambling to his feet in a fury*]: Out of my sight! [*She is gone.*] Out of my – [*He is overcome with sobs. He clamps his teeth against them and closes the door and leans against it, exhausted.*] Oh, my God! God help me! [*Quaking with fear . . .*]. (Miller, 17–18)

Miller's tight control over the scene's emotional and gestural choreography is exercised through the extensive use of square brackets with directions to the actors; by contrast, the freedom for actors encountering Shakespeare's sparse stage directions has meant that his plays have continued to be performed in quite different contexts, settings and styles.

Shakespeare was probably not writing his plays with publication in mind – unlike Miller (the question of whether Shakespeare wrote for publication is a contentious one in Shakespeare scholarship). A modern dramatist can probably expect his or her plays to be more read than seen in performance; the opposite is true for the early modern period, where most plays were never printed, and if they were, the print-run (usually estimated at about 800) is dwarfed by the capacity of the theatres (2,000 to 3,000 audience members at any one performance). Perhaps Shakespeare, as resident dramatist for the King's Men, could expect to be present at rehearsals to indicate in person the specific way in which particular scenes in *Macbeth* ought to be played. Whatever the explanation for the minimal stage directions, we might argue that this light touch has been hugely beneficial to actors and directors over the intervening centuries, free to deliver lines and imagine character and setting without the heavy hand of authorial direction on the text.

There are no indications in the Folio for 'asides' – a non-naturalistic technique in which a character speaks his own thoughts while, apparently, those close to him on stage cannot hear him. Most modern editors indicate that Macbeth's speeches when he hears that he has been made Thane of Cawdor are asides: this direction rarely appears in early modern printed plays, where it seems to have been assumed that if no character on stage responds to what has been said, we accept that it has not been audible to them (the space of the stage need not directly correlate to real space, after all, anymore than the body of the actor correlates to that of the character). Sometimes the play gives us what are sometimes called internal or implicit stage directions. Lady Macbeth breaks her speech with 'Hark, peace: it was the owl that shriek'd' (2.2.3), which may be the indication that the noise of an owl cry was audible in the theatre, although there is no stage direction indicating so (as there is in the preceding scene, with 'A bell rings' (2.1.61SD)). Alternatively, this example may indicate the edgy, hallucinatory atmosphere of the chamber in which the guilty pair think they hear the noises of discovery where we hear nothing but their own panicked words. On occasion we can see that the stage direction is slightly out of sync with the dialogue: where the Folio has the sequence 'What is that noise? [SD] *A cry within of women*. It is the cry of women, my good lord', modern editions place the stage direction a line earlier so that it prompts, rather than follows, the question.

Enter Thomas Middleton

If the editorial questions around *Macbeth* seem relatively straightforward compared to other Shakespeare plays, there is one major issue about the text: the question of revision. Many modern scholars believe that the younger playwright Thomas Middleton, with whom Shakespeare collaborated on the satiric tragedy *Timon of Athens*, probably written just before *Macbeth*, may well have had a hand in the text of *Macbeth* that is printed in the Folio. Middleton is thought to have revised Shakespeare's text, perhaps after Shakespeare retired from the London theatre scene or even after he died.

The reasons for this inference – there is no external evidence of co-authorship or revision – coalesce around scenes with Hecate. Two of the witches' songs are referred to in the Folio text with reference to their opening lines only: 'Come away, come away &c' (3.1.33SD) and 'Blacke Spirits, &c' (4.1.43SD). We know that in the early modern theatre the texts of songs may well have been on separate sheets that were not part of the promptbook copy, and therefore there are a number of occasions where song lyrics have not made it into the printed text, as here. But we also know that another play, Thomas Middleton's *The Witch* (probably written around 1613, but not printed), included songs with the same opening phrases. Adapting Shakespeare's play in the later seventeenth century, William Davenant included the full text of the two songs, suggesting that they were part of the

theatrical tradition of *Macbeth* (Davenant was unlikely to
have known the manuscript of *The Witch*). In addition, the
stage direction formula 'enter X meeting Y' has been identified as distinctive to Middleton: it appears in *Macbeth* at the
beginning of 2.1 and in 3.5. Gary Taylor has suggested that
Middleton wrote about 11 per cent of the text of *Macbeth*
as printed in the Folio (Middleton, 1165) including 3.5 and
parts of 4.1, and, further, that he may have been responsible for cuts to the text that have produced so notably compressed a play (see Chapter Two).

Perhaps Middleton's role was to recast the role and the
appearance of the witches in line with what has been called a
witch-vogue on the Jacobean stage. Simon Forman's account
of them as 'three women fairies or nymphs' when he saw the
play at the Globe in 1611 seems closer to the description in
Holinshed of 'some nymphs or fairies' rather than the bearded
hags of the play, and it may be that the Weird Sisters were originally closer to the goddesses of destiny of the source material.
Many commentators on the Hecate scenes have noticed that
they graft onto a story of village witchcraft in which petty
scores like the withholding of chestnuts are settled through
magic, a more elevated, classical image of the underworld.
Diane Purkiss has identified that 'the witches of *Macbeth* are
a low-budget, frankly exploitative collage of randomly chosen
bits of witch-lore, selected not for thematic significance but
for its sensation value' (Purkiss, 207): Shakespeare was per-
fectly capable of such populist work, but it may also be that
the 'collage' effect of the witches' scenes is the result of later
revision by Middleton.

So, to return to the point where we began: what is the text
with which we are working? The answer is that it is something slightly more unstable than the writing guides might
suggest. We can work from the First Folio text, which has
the advantage of age and priority – it is the earliest extant
version – but cannot claim to be direct from Shakespeare's
quill. Its unfamiliar orthography (spelling) and presentation
also make it more rebarbative to read: those u and v switches

can be surprisingly baffling on the page. Alternatively we can work with one of the modern editions. Quotations in this book, unless otherwise indicated, are from the Arden text, edited by Kenneth Muir and first published in 1951. I am using the *Arden Shakespeare Complete Works* edition which includes a slightly revised version of Muir's text, but a complete new edition is expected soon. If you have access to different editions you will see variations between their versions of *Macbeth*: probably small ones, but nevertheless potentially significant ones, particularly around stage directions, punctuation and spelling. Some import those Middleton songs from *The Witch*; others leave the opening phrases as found in the Folio.

The text of *Macbeth*, like the text of any Shakespeare play, is in a kind of flux – originating in a time before the standardization of spelling, presentation and copy editing we have come to expect of a printed book, and, importantly, before our idolization of the genius of Shakespeare. That text has been redrawn over subsequent ages according to contemporary expectations about Shakespeare and contemporary assessments of literary merit – that's why there are so many different editions of Shakespeare and why the major modern series – the Arden, Oxford, Norton and Cambridge – are engaged in permanent cycles of revision and re-editing. Further, the text of a play is always more than a script on a page: unlike a novel or a poem, a play does not have its primary life in print, and thus the role of production, actual and potential, also needs to be taken into account.

Perhaps all we can hope, then, is to be as aware as possible of the editor's role in shaping the text, and to refer back to the Folio or out to alternative versions to get a sense of the different interpretative possibilities. The text, like our readings of it, is plural and playful – a dynamic range of meanings rather than right or wrong answers. Like editors, critics, actors and directors, that's to say, we as readers will draw our own versions of *Macbeth* in the pages ahead.

Reading *Macbeth* 1.7.1–28

Having discussed the text of *Macbeth* in rather distant and editorial terms above, let's now – it's not an entirely happy figure of speech for the play – get our hands dirty. This section will focus on Macbeth's soliloquy in 1.7, when he contemplates the killing of Duncan. The aim is to develop some close-reading techniques alongside some insights from contemporary actors, in order to understand how Shakespeare's language can convey emotion, subtext and meaning.

To put the speech in the context of the play: so far, we have encountered the witches' prophecies to Macbeth and Banquo, the award of the thaneship of Cawdor to Macbeth on the treachery of its prior holder, and Lady Macbeth's dramatic reaction to her husband's letter. In 1.6, Lady Macbeth welcomes King Duncan to Dunsinane castle, which he praises to his 'fair and noble hostess' (1.6.24) as 'a pleasant seat' whose air 'nimbly and sweetly recommends itself/Unto our gentle senses' (1.6.1–3). Banquo suggests the castle must be frequented by 'the temple-haunting martlet' – either a swift or a house-martin, migrant summer birds (1.6.4). Their words resound heavily: we already know that Lady Macbeth has responded to her husband's report of the witches' prophecy by summoning a bird with quite different, more gothic connotations, the ominous 'raven [. . .]/That croaks the fatal entrance of Duncan/Under my battlements' (1.5.37–9). The Cheek by Jowl theatre company production in 2010 presented Duncan as a blind man, literalizing the sense of misprision that hangs over his arrival at Dunsinane.

Lady Macbeth promises that 'He that's coming/Must be provided for' (1.5.65–6): her words echo with menace, since the providing that she anticipates is not the comfort and hospitality that might be expected. 'Provide', according to the Oxford English Dictionary, has as its earliest meaning 'to foresee' or 'to make provision for the future'. The future Lady Macbeth foresees for Duncan is no future at all: 'never/Shall sun that

morrow see!' (1.5.59–60). That the future is no future is one
of the play's great existential discoveries (think of 'To-morrow
and to-morrow and to-morrow' (5.5.19), words which ought
to resonate with potential but which come to beat out empty,
meaningless repetition) and here the word 'provided' resounds
with some of the play's preoccupation with the past, present
and future tenses of action. 'It's an amazing line,' Sinead
Cusack, Lady Macbeth in Adrian Noble's 1986 production,
explains: 'She's going to play hostess to Duncan at Dunsinane
and "provide" is what gracious hostesses always do. It's a wonder of a line to play because the reverberations do the acting
for you, make the audience go "Aaagh?"' (Rutter, 62).

The arrival of the king to Dunsinane establishes one of the
surprising features of *Macbeth*: its domesticity, which will be
discussed in more detail below. Much of the play takes place
inside, behind the closed doors of the castle to which such
attention is drawn in the porter's scene (2.3) and to which the
stormed castle of Macduff is a poignant parallel. When Lady
Macduff talks of the 'the poor wren,/The most diminutive of
birds, will fight,/Her young ones in her nest, against the owl'
(4.2.9–11) the imagery from nature is telling: home should
be a safe haven. Macbeth's acknowledgement that he should
protect Duncan as his sovereign and his guest – 'as his host/
Who should against his murtherer shut the door,/Not bear
the knife myself' (1.7.15–6) – has something of the spookiness
of Emily Dickinson's short poem:

Far safer through an Abbey gallop,
The stones achase,
Than, moonless, one's own self encounter
In lonesome place.

Ourself, behind ourself concealed,
Should startle most;
Assassin, hid in our apartment,
Be horror's least.

The prudent carries a revolver,
He bolts the door,

O'erlooking a superior spectre
More near.

Dickinson's poem articulates the way in which our fears attach themselves to external objects when really they are always and already within: less the gothic terrors of the ruined abbey or the modern worry of a burgled apartment, and more the uncanny encounter with 'one's own self', that 'superior spectre/More near'. Her word 'assassin' echoes with Shakespeare's 'assassination' (she was greatly influenced by the play, and references in her letters show her familiarity with its language and her particular fascination with the character of Lady Macbeth). The irony, is, of course, as Macbeth comes to see, that like Duncan he too is trapped with the murderer: himself. In his 1948 film, Orson Welles has the shadow of Macbeth fall across the image of the sleeping Duncan: it is an object of menace to Macbeth more than to his unconscious victim.

All this establishes Macbeth's first sustained soliloquy which opens the next scene in an atmosphere of ironized domesticity. The stage direction which opens 1.7 establishes, aurally and visually, a context of festivity against which Macbeth's dark speech unfolds. 'Ho-boyes. Torches. Enter a Sewer, and divers Servants with Dishes and Service over the stage. Then enter Macbeth'. 'Ho-boyes' or wood instruments that were the forerunners of oboes were the stage's musical cue for banqueting; the 'Sewer' is a butler or attendant at elaborate meals, and the specific detail of dishes and service passing across the stage indicate the busy work behind the scenes of the King's reception. The music and stage business thus perform a wholesome version of Lady Macbeth's promise of provision – Duncan *is* being provided for – against which the other meaning is juxtaposed. Macbeth's own language shows his thoughts run darker:

If it were done when 'tis done, then 'twere well
It were done quickly: if th'assassination
Could trammel up the consequence, and catch

With his surcease, success; that but this blow
Might be the be-all and the end-all – here,   5
But here, upon this bank and shoal of time,
We'd jump the life to come. – But in these cases,
We still have judgement here; that we but teach
Bloody instructions, which, being taught, return
To plague th'inventor: this even-handed justice   10
Commends th'ingredience of our poison'd chalice
To our own lips. He's here in double trust:
First, as I am his kinsman, and his subject,
Strong both against the deed; then, as his host,
Who should against his murtherer shut the door,   15
Not bear the knife myself. Besides, this Duncan
Hath borne his faculties so meek, hath been
So clear in his great office, that his virtues
Will plead like angels, trumpet-tongu'd, against
The deep damnation of his taking-off;   20
And Pity, like a naked new-born babe,
Striding the blast, or heaven's Cherubins, hors'd
Upon the sightless couriers of the air,
Shall blow the horrid deed in every eye,
That tears shall drown the wind. I have no spur   25
To prick the sides of my intent, but only
Vaulting ambition, which o'erleaps itself
And falls on th'other. (1.7.1–28)

The first and most important thing to say about this speech
is it is difficult, at least in part because it captures Macbeth's
own profound difficulty. No one listening to it at the Globe
could have caught more than a few flashes of understanding of specific phrases and an overall impression of mental angst. No analysis can or should try to explain what it
'means' or translate it into simpler terms, because its main
purpose is to record complexity. The language is in excess
of its meaning, or, to paraphrase Samuel Beckett's insight
discussed in the introduction, the language is the meaning,
'the thing itself'.

One way to make sense of this complexity, however, is to psychologize it. Macbeth does not express himself clearly, either because he cannot, since he is not himself clear about his purpose here, or because he will not, because he won't face up to or publicize his own desires. 'Thou wouldst be great,' said Lady Macbeth, 'Art not without ambition, but without/ The illness should attend it' (1.5.17–9). Macbeth's speech opens without ever stating what it is about. Pronouns stand in for the absent nouns; euphemisms take the place of directness. Simon Palfrey discusses the triple repetition of 'done' in the opening phrase and remarks on its 'curious mixture of bluntness and evasion': the repetition 'has the paradoxical effect of both reinforcement and weakening. Most importantly, it makes the words "hang" in the air, as though in the very space of Macbeth's present form' (Palfrey, 67). For Palfrey the repetition slows down the moment like a mental freeze-frame, rather as the theatre director John Barton advises actors: 'when a Shakespearean speech is in monosyllables it's always good counsel not to rush it. Each word needs to breathe, so take your time' (Barton, 98). Against this sense of hesitation is the competing feeling that the speech moves headlong. On performing the soliloquy, Derek Jacobi noted that 'Macbeth's mind is working with enormous speed, and I wanted to reflect that in the speaking; he is thinking very rapidly, and the time, and thought and speech come simultaneously' (Jacobi, 194). 'Time for further thought is hardly available, however: if Duncan is to be killed, it must be done that night. The swiftness of the time-scheme is reflected in the swiftness of the language. Sometimes it is almost telegrammatic. The actor will wish to get his point across, his interpretation of a particular line, but it's not always easy because it's all so densely written. There may well be six images in a line and have you have to choose only one or two – you can't do them all, you can't play everything' (Jacobi, 199–200).

One noticeable feature of Macbeth's soliloquy here is his inability to name the deed he contemplates. The witches later will claim that they do 'a deed without a name' (4.1.49): but

that namelessness is anticipated here. The deed that is con-
templated is so terrible as to be unnameable. We can see that
Macbeth begins his speech here with pronouns rather than
nouns: 'If it were done when 'tis done' begins without the
noun to which "it" refers.' In part we catch his thought here
in mid-flow, as if he is continuing an internal conversation
begun when he left Lady Macbeth with the words 'We will
speak further' at 1.5.70. Simon Palfrey brilliantly notices
that even the pronouns here are repeatedly elided, caught up
in the following syllable as indicated by the apostrophe, as
if to speed over them as quickly as is verbally and syntactically possible: 'tis', 'twere' (Palfrey, 67). The language here
is tongue-twisting: dense, bristling with consonants, difficult
to speak: try reading it aloud to experience this. When the
deferred noun comes it is so unusual as to be another kind
of euphemism. It sounds different, for one thing: after a
sequence of 13 consecutive monosyllables, often associated
with words of English etymology, in lines 1–2, its polysyllabic
form marks out its more learned register. 'Assassination' is not
recorded before its usage here: it derives from 'assassin', originally a word for Muslim fighters in the Crusades and literally
a hashish-eater (*OED*). The sound and meaning of the word
are strange, and so too is its referent: this is an alienating term
both in the sense that it implicitly likens Macbeth's plan to
something done by exotic and distant people, and in the sense
that the word itself is likely to have been opaque to most of
the play's first listeners.

Macbeth both explains, then, and obscures his meaning,
just as the repeated use of 'but' or 'besides' as conjunctions
makes his argument proceed by negatives and contractions.
Each attempt to quieten or still his thought prompts another
to bubble up: the speech is made up of long, inconclusive
sentences which attempt closure but are immediately reanimated. The syntax thus enacts that impossibility of finality
with which the speech opens: 'but that this blow/Might be the
be-all and the end-all'. There can be no mental 'surcease' ('that
action, or an act, of bringing or coming to an end', *OED*),

another word, this time from the legal world, that is marked with strangeness. Michael Goldman's account of Macbeth's habitual habit of verbal 'smothering' is helpful here: 'Balances are set up which are quickly undermined by unassimilated residues of sound and sense, and this makes the movement from word . . . to word . . . neither one of opposition nor simple accumulation, but of a twisting and darkening, a thickening in which the speech thrusts forward into little thickets of sound and into reflections which don't allow the speculative movement to exist, ending literally in a smothering negation' (Goldman, 95). It's striking how Goldman's terms here come from the play itself and its own lexis of thickening, darkening and negation: 'nothing is, but what is not' (1.3.142).

The pattern of juxtaposing elaborate, polysyllabic vocabulary with more everyday and simple language is a feature of *Macbeth* throughout (think of the explanation of 'multitudinous seas incarnadine' as 'making the green one red' (2.2.61–2)). It used to be seen as one of its failures of decorum, as discussed below. It continues through this speech. Like 'assassination', 'consequence' seems to function as a euphemism. Macbeth seems caught up in the sounds of his words as an escape from their true meaning: rolling 'surcease, success' and 'the be-all and the end-all'. These half-rhymes suggest a kind of deceptively comforting logic as he struggles to make sense of the senseless moment of indecision. He turns to generalizations – 'the bank and shoal of time', 'this even-handed justice' – and to the evasive second-person 'we' (there are only two instances of the first person 'I' in these 27 lines, an index of how difficult Macbeth finds it to own his obliquely expressed desires here). Metaphors and associations build further to obscure the underlying meaning: 'trammel' and 'bank' have associations with fishing, 'trammel' and 'jump' with horses, later extended with 'horsed' and 'spur', but 'jump' and 'horsed' may also suggest a gymnastic vaulting-horse, hence 'vaulting ambition'. 'Ingredience' placed in conjunction with 'chalice' has eucharistic associations, as well as a suggestion of medicine, or poison (the sickness of the state and of the humans is an important theme in the play). Religion is clearly invoked with 'angels', 'heaven's cherubins'.

'Blow' is both the noise of the trumpet, the action of the 'wind', and a stroke or punch: this simple word gained a particular prominence in the aftermath of the Gunpowder Plot, since 'blow' was a hidden clue in an intercepted letter about the conspiracy and reportedly the hint deciphered by James himself. Gary Willis, who has written extensively on the play's relation to this event, writes that 'wordplay on the various forms of "blow" would be common in accounts of the Plot or references to it' (Willis, 20). 'Blow', then, is also an allusion to the killing of a king (the aim of the Gunpowder Plot), but in keeping with the rest of Macbeth's speech it cannot acknowledge that desire, that 'horrid deed'. That this is a speech about an anticipated murder is clear from its context, but not from its content. Mentions of violence are allusive rather than explicit: the 'bloody instructions', the 'poisoned chalice', the 'knife'. The murder is literally unspeakable, disguised as 'assassination', 'consequence', 'the deed', 'the horrid deed'. Duncan is not to be killed but to undergo a 'taking-off': the word 'murderer' does break in but is distanced by the use of the third person: at this point, at least syntactically, the murderer is still another person, but not for long.

Jacobi suggests that the imagery of the speech reflects Macbeth's own nature: 'His head is full of the mixture of good and evil. At this moment, the evil side of him, which we all possess, is getting the upper hand, and in order to balance it he brings up the best, the purest, the most innocent images, or angels, and new-born babies, and the sky. They are all pure, unsullied, wonderful images; goodness pours out of them; they're shining. And on the other side are the dark, blood-driven, evil, dank thoughts' (Jacobi, 201). Following this performance insight we might draw up a list of words under each of these headings – 'justice', 'chalice', 'trust', 'meek', clear', 'virtues'; 'assassination', 'poisoned', 'murderer', 'knife', 'damnation'. But what also emerges is a number of more abstract words whose immediate connotations are neither good nor evil, or which have a capacity for both. The etymology of the word 'host' denotes both 'host' and 'stranger' (the word 'hostile' comes from the same root); 'ambition' has both positive and negative associations. Clustering the words according to their ethical charge reveals the difficulty of understanding Macbeth's speech here as a simple struggle between impulses to good and to evil.

It is often claimed that Shakespeare's vocabulary was the largest of any English writer. In fact David Crystal has estimated a working vocabulary of around 20,000 different words in Shakespeare's plays, compared with an active vocabulary of more than twice that number that he assesses for modern English speakers. Shakespeare's vocabulary is large for the time – considerably larger than that of the King James Bible, for instance, which is about the same length as the Shakespeare corpus – but not particularly large by modern standards. And estimates of Shakespeare's contribution to the language in coining new words have been downscaled as more early modern texts are searchable on the internet, although it still seems that Shakespeare is the first recorded author to use around 1,700 words in the *OED*. What is striking, and inventive, about Shakespeare's language is its flexibility: the ease with which he presses nouns into service as verbs or vice versa, or compounds words together in new and newly poetic ways. A concordance is a list of words and where they appear in Shakespeare's plays and can help us identify what's unusual about a given play or word. Online texts make it much easier for us to search for multiple instances of the same word in a play, giving us a kind of linguistic heat map showing how its themes and plot are advanced at the level of individual words.

Performing such a search can help us to draw some verbal connections between this speech and the rest of the play. Certain words accrete meaning through repetition. 'Double', for instance, features here: 'he's here in double trust', but it gains negative connotations as the play unfolds, particularly in its repeated formulation 'Double, double' in the witches' spell (4.1.10). Almost all the uses of this work have negative connotations, culminating in Macbeth's recognition of the witches' 'double sense' (5.8.20). 'Deed', used twice in this scene, recurs as the preferred term for the murder of Duncan: 'th'attempt and not the deed/Confounds us', reports Lady Macbeth, as she returns drunk with the excitement of drugging Duncan's grooms (2.2.10–11). 'I have done the deed', is Macbeth's heavy confession as he brings back the bloody daggers (2.2.14). 'A little water clears us of this deed', she counsels (2.2.66): 'To know my deed, 'twere best not know myself' is Macbeth's reply (2.2.72). But the word not only belongs to the murderous couple. The Old Man reports on things 'unnatural/Even like the deed that's done' (2.4.10–11), as the natural world revolts at Duncan's murder. Ross asks 'is't known who did this more than bloody deed' (2.4.22), and Macduff replies that Duncan's sons Malcolm and Donalbain are in 'suspicion of the deed' (2.4.27). Macbeth vows to do the 'deed' of eliminating Macduff's family (4.1.154) but urges his wife 'be innocent . . . Till thou applaud the deed' (3.2.45–6). The 'deed' functions for the play as an alternative to the word 'murder': its etymology suggests agency or responsibility – a 'deed' is, by definition, something that has been 'done' by someone – even as the syntax of its use tends to try to evade such responsibility or leave it unspoken: Macbeth's 'my deed' (2.2.72) is unusual in its acknowledgement of agency.

Doing a similar search for the play's uses of the word 'time', or 'door', 'hand' or 'against' helps us to see how the play knits together its linguistic fabric, and how the language of the play intersects with the particular language-use of its characters. Similarly, we can get a sense of words that are unusual in the speech. 'Be-all and end-all' is Shakespeare's coinage here: it would have struck the first audiences as a new phrase rather than the familiar quotation we may now recognize. 'Assassination' and 'ingredience' do not appear elsewhere in Shakespeare; 'surcease', 'courier/s', occurs in three other plays, 'cherubins' in two. The thought processes here are unusual, and so too is the vocabulary in which they are expressed.

Rhythm and metre

We have focused so far on language and word-choice. Thinking about the rhythm and structure of the speech gives us a different way to analyse its ethical and linguistic contortions. We know that Shakespeare's habitual rhythm was iambic pentameter, basically a ten-syllable line with five stressed beats. In its standard form the metre is unstressed–stressed, hence *iambic* (an unstressed syllable followed by a stressed one, as in 'to-DAY'). Macbeth's first line in the play, 'So fair and foul a day I have not seen' (1.3.38), follows this pattern: 'so FAIR and FOUL a DAY I HAVE not SEEN': ten regular iambs, which we can hear clearly because all the words are monosyllables and because the syntactic unit of the sentence is the same as the metrical unit of the line.

For the most part, though, whatever guides to Shakespeare's verse would have us believe, the rhythms of the plays are more varied and less rigid than this outline would suggest. For one thing, a singsong rhythm would quickly be boring over the 2,500 lines of the play. Early modern audiences were adept at listening, both to content and to rhythm. 'I suppose their response to the beat', writes the veteran voice coach at the Royal Shakespeare Company Cicely Berry, 'would have been as instinctive as a modern audience listening to rock or reggae or jazz: we know when it is consistent with the message, we very often pick up on the humour in the rhythm, and we know when it is broken' (Berry, 53). Like rap artists and jazz musicians, Shakespeare understood the dramatic power of varying the rhythm, and of frustrating expectations of what might come next. There are lots of examples where, for instance, the first syllable of a line is stressed. Lady Macbeth's 'Glamis thou art, and Cawdor; and shalt be' (1.5.14) would be stressed 'GLAMIS thou ART and CAWdor AND shalt BE' – we can see the stress pattern is unexpected but that it forces attention onto certain words, particularly the second AND. Lady Macbeth's line stresses works to naturalize the next step of the prophecy: since you're already Thane of Glamis and Cawdor (stressing those two names), you will also be . . .' (like her husband, she cannot quite name what: 'What thou art promised'): the stress on the word 'and' actually works. Similarly, a stress on 'BE' makes it into an imperative.

And there are other lines where the stress is dependent on an actor's understanding of the line. If 'Is this a dagger, which I see before me' (2.1.33) is a conventional iambic pentameter line, the stress in the opening words should fall 'Is THIS'. Certainly, that's a possible reading of the line, which emphasizes the materiality of the vision to Macbeth (and the fact that we cannot see it). But we could also imagine an actor delivering the words 'IS this', where the initial stress works to focus us on his questioning incredulity: is this vision real or not? Something similar happens in the soliloquy in 1.7: 'If it were done when 'tis done, then 'twere well'. We could stress this as 'If IT were DONE when TIS done, THEN 'twere WELL': these stresses make prominent the evaded thing itself – 'it' – and the first verb 'done', and as a sequence those stressed words 'it done 'tis then well' stand as a pointed summary of the longer line. But an actor might choose to stress the opening 'IF it WERE', a conditional repeated in the second line of the speech, which would emphasize the way the speech opens on contingency and uncertainty. Shakespeare's metre is an art, not a science, and often the lines have different intonational possibilities if you look at them closely.

Cicely Berry has extensive experience helping actors make sense of Shakespeare's language to themselves and to modern audiences, and often the games and techniques actors use can unlock different, more physical responses to the plays. One consequence of the structure of iambic pentameter is that the words move forwards – each unstressed syllable precedes and topples into a stressed syllable – and so the line is eager to get to the next important emphasis. This is true of Shakespeare's plays generally, but, as the discussion of speed and time Chapter Two identifies, this headlong movement has particular purchase in this most speedy and hurtling of plays.

In turn, the standard stress-pattern of iambic pentamenter throws particular emphasis on the final word of each line.

Berry suggests reading down the right-hand margin of a verse speech to get a sense of its crucial concerns. For Macbeth's soliloquy in 1.7 that would give us well, assassination, catch, blow, here, time, cases, teach, return, justice, chalice, trust, subject, host, door, Duncan. Up to about half-way through the speech, that's to say, the final word of each line is deeply significant to its overall movement, and if we had only these words and nothing else of the speech, we would have a clear sense of what it is about. After this point the pattern seems to break down: been, virtues, against, taking-off, babe, horsed, air, eye, spur, only, itself. It's much more difficult to get a sense from these words of what's going on, just as the metaphors of the second half of the speech become more confused and confusing. Berry herself puts it this way: 'as the speech progresses the line endings become less defined, and this reinforces the sense that [Macbeth's] thoughts get out of control' (Berry, 86). One variation on this technique is to use the first and last words of each line as a kind of verbal ladder to understand the direction and thrust of a speech.

Macbeth's speech, then, is a meditation around, rather than on, its subject. In its course it touches on a theme that the play will elsewhere develop: the 'naked new-born babe' has its echo in the children, literal and figurative, that stalk the play-world (see Chapter Three). It establishes Duncan as a figure of moral strength who is 'so clear in his great office', and thus raises the stakes of Macbeth's betrayal even as the idea coalesces in his mind. Inevitably, because it dramatizes the irresolution and uncertainty, the speech ends anticlimactically as its language begins to falter: the imagery, like the rhythm of the speech itself, is of falling. 'To prick the sides of my intent, but only' is a line with an extra syllable. The final '-ly' dissipates the line's force, so that the metre follows the sense, o'erleaping itself to fall. Lady Macbeth's entrance interrupts the speech's diminuendo.

This speech, then, is structured by opacity, by a language that obscures meaning through euphemism, extended and interconnected metaphor and wordplay. We may expect that a character who comes alone on stage to talk to the audience intends to communicate clearly with us. Patsy Rodenburg tells actors that 'through soliloquy, characters invite the audience inside their heads, to witness their motives. Soliloquy is only written for characters who have no one else to speak to. The audience is their only friend and confidante. They test their ideas with us through soliloquy; and as soon as they have found out what to do they cease speaking to us' (Rodenburg, 2002: 222). She may well be right – it's how Hamlet, for example, seems to use soliloquy, or Iago in *Othello* – but it's a view of soliloquy that doesn't quite work for *Macbeth*. Macbeth's speech here does not treat us his friend and confidante; the speech is marked instead by evasion and solipsism. Most early modern soliloquies would have been directly delivered to the audience, unlike the modern technique in filmed Shakespeare where soliloquies tend to be given as voice-overs with a close-up on the actor's intense expression and unmoving lips (as in, for example, Roman Polanski's brutal 1971 film). But Macbeth seems here to be talking to himself more in the manner of the film soliloquy than to an audience. Deictic words – ones that gain meaning through context, such as 'here' or 'this' – in the speech refer to the illusory world of the play, not to the real, material space of the theatre. There is no sense of a shared space or shared experience: the second-person 'we' does not seem to assert commonality with the audience. Macbeth is on his own. We can watch and listen, peer into the abyss. What is most troubling about this play is that we can only be, but not know, Macbeth.

Without fear?

Having looked at the speech in this detail, you are in a good position to analyse the following:

MACBETH: If this business would really be finished when I did the deed, then it would be best to get it over with quickly. If the assassination of the king could work like a net, sweeping up everything and preventing any consequences, then the murder would be the be-all and end-all of the whole affair and I would gladly put my soul and the afterlife at risk to do it. But for crimes like these there are still punishments in this world. By committing violent crimes we only teach other people to commit violence, and the violence of our students will come back to plague us teachers. Justice, being equal to everyone, forces us to drink from the poisoned cup that we serve to others. The king trusts me in two ways. First of all, I am his kinsman and his subject, so I should always try to protect him. Second, I am his host, so I should be closing the door in his murderer's face, not trying to murder him myself. Besides, Duncan has been such a humble leader, so free of corruption, that his virtuous legacy will speak for him when he dies, as if angels were playing trumpets against the injustice of his murder. Pity, like an innocent newborn baby, will ride the wind with winged angels on invisible horses through the air to spread news of the horrible deed to everyone everywhere. People will shed a flood of tears that will drown the wind like a horrible downpour of rain. I can't spur myself to action. The only thing motivating me is ambition, which makes people rush ahead of themselves toward disaster.

This translation of the speech from SparkNotes is under their 'No Fear Shakespeare' tab. It's a useful and potentially helpful tool for beginners. But perhaps it registers a misapprehension about the purposes of Shakespeare's difficulty. Should our reading of this play of horrors be without fear? 'Fear', 'fears', 'afraid' and 'fearful' are part of the very texture of the play: the words occur more than 50 times. Macbeth's numbness as the play proceeds translates into the difference between experiencing fear – 'that suggestion/Whose horrid image doth

unfix my hair,/And make my seated heart knock at my ribs'
(1.3.134–6) – to his final indifference. By the play's conclusion
he has so 'supped full of horrors' that he has 'almost forgot
the taste of fears' (5.5.9, 5.5.14). To be without fear in the
play is to be inhuman, to be pretending to be alive rather than
really living. *Macbeth* without fear would be a pale creature,
since the play explores and evokes the emotion so completely.
Fear is part of the excitement the play produces.

But have a look again at the SparkNotes version of the
speech: does it explain anything you didn't already discern
about what Macbeth is saying? It is 20 per cent longer than
Shakespeare and less precise, but through repetition it also
registers that many of his phrases are already clearly comprehensible: 'be-all and the end-all', 'first, as I am his kinsman
and his subject'. Sometimes words that have double meanings
are resolved into one: Shakespeare's 'sightless' is here 'invisible' when it also evokes 'blind'; 'two ways' loses the echo with
'double'; 'bank and shoal of time' goes completely. Certain
interpolations are questionable: SparkNotes' Macbeth often
generalizes: 'everyone everywhere' is weaker than the strangely
disembodied 'every eye' in the play; 'people rush ahead of
themselves' is again less uncanny, less possessed than the personified 'vaulting ambition, which o'erleaps itself'. SparkNotes
names Duncan's 'murder', which, as we have seen, Shakespeare
delicately evades. Their 'horrible downpour of rain' – a rather
bathetic image is offered as a simile for the more densely meta-
phoric 'tears shall drown the wind': the strangeness of that
image in the play conveys Macbeth's loosening grip on his
thought processes. And 'I can't spur myself to action' seems
a misreading of 'I have no spur . . . but . . .': Macbeth says his
only spur is ambition, rather than that he has no spur. So the
gains of clarity here are at a cost.

The point of all this is not a cheap gibe at SparkNotes –
great tagline: 'when your books and teachers don't make
sense, we do' – but an encouragement to you: you don't need it.
Shakespeare's speech is untranslatable, and its difficulties are
intrinsic, not incidental. But the speech is also deeply enjoyable

and memorable, not in spite, but because of, its complexity. No one, not Macbeth himself, quite understands what he's saying. How could we, since what he is doing is at one level so deeply inexplicable? Part of reading Shakespeare involves leaving behind notions of direct translation and responding to the words as we might to music, or to visual art: as something that *is*, first, and *means*, second.

Review of 1.7

So far in this chapter we have deployed a range of techniques to discuss a single speech – Macbeth's soliloquy in 1.7 – and to understand why the particular form in which it is written, and in particular its word-choice and rhythms, is inseparable from the dense range of associative meanings we can get from its analysis. Thinking about how the words set off associations with other language-use in the play reminds us that this speech is part of a dynamic of action as well as a poetic set-piece, and using some of the exercises devised for Shakespearean actors reminds us that the range of poetic meanings we can derive in the study need to have their corollary in the theatre.

Macbeth and the domestic

The final section of this chapter develops a broader theme out of some of the suggestions of Macbeth's speech, to illustrate how the context and register of individual moments in the play contribute to the whole.

We have already noticed the specificity of the stage-setting: 'Ho-boyes. Torches. Enter a Sewer, and divers Servants with Dishes and Service over the stage. Then enter Macbeth' (1.7.0SD). Unusually the stage direction here indicates a sequence of business which is not directly required by the speech that follows it: it serves simply to bring to life the off-stage space of the celebratory feast from which Macbeth, tortured by his restless mind, has escaped. (We see something similar when the bloody daggers work to evoke the unstaged scene of Duncan's murder.) But the stage direction also works to provide a visual reminder of something Macbeth's speech, and Macbeth's character, both struggle with: this is not a battlefield but a domestic home; Macbeth is not a soldier but a host; Duncan is not an enemy but a guest; unseaming from the nave to the chops might be appropriate in armed conflict but is an outrage at home. In a number of his plays Shakespeare tackles the difficulty for the male hero in reducing himself to the constraints of private, domestic life. Here in *Macbeth* this domestic world is evoked most insistently through the play's language.

As we saw in the discussion of the word 'assassination' above, *Macbeth* has its fair share of neologisms (new words) and words that would have sounded unfamiliar to contemporary audiences. Words such as 'multitudinous' (only otherwise found in the contemporaneous play *Coriolanus*), 'compunctious', 'incarnadine', 'parricide', 'purveyor' and 'dis-seat' are examples of polysyllabic coinages and elevated diction unique to this play. If we look at these words in their context in *Macbeth* they tend to display mental effort or evasion: characters attempting to give voice to thoughts that are difficult or abnormal often struggle with a peculiar vocabulary. But these are not the only kinds of words found in the play. Many critics have noticed, and some have disapproved of, the mingling in *Macbeth* of words from an elevated, multisyllabic or Latinate register with those of a more bathetic or mundane sort. When Macbeth calls his wife 'dearest chuck', for instance, he uses a term of endearment which is all the more striking because of its context:

> Be innocent of the knowledge, dearest chuck,
> Till thou applaud the deed. Come, seeling Night,
> Scarf up the tender eye of pitiful Day,
> And with thy bloody and invisible hand,
> Cancel, and tear to pieces, that great bond
> Which keeps me pale! (3.2.45–50)

Macbeth's language shifts dizzyingly from the playful, private dialogue of family intimacy into an evocation of a monstrously personified Night, whose hands are as bloody as his own. The change of tone is a linguistic one: the moment opens an existential chasm under the everyday world. It is a destabilizing manoeuvre typical of the language of the play.

One notable example of diction thought inappropriately ordinary is found in Lady Macbeth's invocation to the 'Spirits/ That tend on mortal thoughts' to 'unsex me here' (1.5.39–40). Her invitation to the powers of darkness to suppress her femininity anticipates Macbeth's 'come, seeling night' as it concludes:

> Come, thick Night,
> And pall thee in the dunnest smoke of Hell,
> That my keen knife see not the wound it makes,
> Nor Heaven peep through the blanket of the dark,
> To cry, 'Hold, hold!' (1.5.49–53)

Samuel Johnson, one of Shakespeare's earliest commentators suggested that the imagery here was inadvertently amusing: 'who, without some relaxation of his gravity, can hear of the avengers of guilt peeping through a blanket' (Johnson, 11). Editors proposed various emendations to smooth out this perceived lapse in taste and tragic decorum: 'blankness', 'blankest', blank height' or 'blackness' were offered as more suitable (Furness, 57–60). Other eighteenth-century readers felt that the word 'knife' was inappropriately domestic as an implement of terror (compared with, say, 'dagger'). Dr Johnson again: 'we do not immediately conceive that any crime of importance is to be committed with a knife' (Johnson, 10).

The commentary is revealing in its implicit sense of what language is appropriate to tragedy. Indeed, that the language and tone appropriate to tragedy is noble and serious was a commonplace of early modern descriptions of the genre (Smith). The Elizabethan theorist George Puttenham argued that writing of highborn individuals, such as tragedy, is 'matter stately and high, and requires a style to be lift up and advanced by choice of words, phrases, sentences, and figures, high, lofty, eloquent, and magnific in proportion'. The courtier Philip Sidney described the 'high and excellent Tragedy' and praised the Tudor play *Gorboduc* for its 'stately speeches and well-sounding phrases, climbing to the height of Seneca's style'. Thomas Heywood quoted Ovid: 'Omne genus scripti gravitate tragœdia vincit' ('In solemn grandeur tragedy is unrivalled'). In all these examples, tragedy is associated with elevated language or with dignity and an imagery of height or distinction: linguistic style is as significant as narrative content in distinguishing genre. The eighteenth-century commentators cited above are heirs to these linguistic assumptions. But *Macbeth*'s deliberate shift of registers, from the mundane to the sublime, recapitulates in microcosm the themes of the play.

Let's take 'blanket', Lady Macbeth's image for the covering that will protect her from the sight of Heaven. As a domestic item it is manifestly at odds with the language of spirits and darkness, but its everydayness anticipates the murder of Duncan in his bed, and the consequences of the murder which see both Macbeth and Lady Macbeth robbed of sleep. Blankets have been reassigned from everyday purposes – what Cleanth Brooks calls 'the clothing of sleep' (Wain, 190) – and put in the service of murder. We could say something similar about the 'knife'. A few moments later, Macbeth also uses the word 'knife', arguing, as we saw in the analysis above, that he should, as 'host', protect Duncan against a murderer rather than 'bear the knife myself' (1.7.14–16). It is precisely the domestic connotations that are relevant. Macbeth's language is of the contradiction between the obligations of hospitality and his own murderous thoughts, as he contemplates committing regicide in his own home. The everyday connotations of the knife, suddenly deployed in this fantasy of murder, underline the perversion of domesticity that is at the heart of the play. This reading is brought to life in the *Shakespeare Retold* (2005) television drama based on the play, which takes place in a restaurant and features its sous-chef Joe Macbeth slicing meat with sinister ease.

In her landmark study of Shakespeare's imagery, Caroline Spurgeon noted Macbeth's 'continuous use made of the simplest, humblest, everyday things, drawn from the daily life in a small house, as a vehicle for sublime poetry' (Spurgeon, 324): perhaps we could modify this insight to acknowledge that the everyday and the sublime are in a productive tension throughout the play. In Rupert Goold's 2008 production, the taps of the washbasin in which Macbeth soaks his guilty hands run red with blood, and as he briefs the murderers about their mission to kill Banquo, he makes a thick sandwich, hacking the bread with a sharp knife in the castle's cold, marbled and stainless steel kitchen. In coupling the ordinary and the horrific, both these directorial inventions serve as visual corollaries of the play's characteristic linguistic habit of juxtaposition.

Just as Lady Macbeth's proverbial 'like the poor cat i'th'adage' – the cat who wanted fish but didn't want to get its feet wet (1.7.45) – uses a trite reference to belittle her husband's new determination to 'proceed no further in this business' (1.7.31), so too mundane or everyday language and props are deployed deliberately and to pointed effect. Something similar happens when Lady Macbeth's clumsy response to the discovery of Duncan's body – 'What! in our house?' (2.3.86) – captures the deep and irretrievable disruption of normality that has occurred. She speaks more than she intends here: the house, the domestic sphere, the relationship of husband and wife, are collateral damage from the murder of the king. Both partners have their differently guilty consciences prosaically conveyed: they cannot sleep peacefully. The place in which Macbeth should feel most comfortable is a torment: he has destroyed his own domestic space in murdering the king. Lady Macbeth is confined to the domestic space throughout; Macbeth apparently never leaves it after the murder of the king, sending murderous emissaries to dispatch Banquo, Fleance and the family of Macduff and preferring to direct the approaching battle with Malcolm's forces from within Dunsinane: 'our castle's strength/Will laugh a siege to scorn' (5.5.2–3). The playworld narrows to the interior of the castle, with Macbeth and Lady Macbeth each effectively confined to their separate chambers. Writing of the 2005 production directed by John Caird, Simon Russell Beale who played Macbeth recalls that at the end they chose to 'present him as almost wholly inactive, waiting for the enemy, waiting for the prophecies to be fulfilled, waiting for the future to come to him. He sat, huge and immobile, in a large chair' (Dobson, 117). Hearing of Fleance's escape from the murderers, Macbeth describes himself 'cabin'd, cribb'd, confin'd, bound in/To saucy doubts and fears' (3.4.23–4): it is the psychological equivalent of this physical constraint.

Domestic tragedy

Emrys Jones likens the play to 'chamber music', 'so long as the term suggested intense concision rather than smallness of scale or narrowness of scope' (Jones, 197), but the spatial, interior dimension of his analogy is also relevant. *Macbeth*'s use of everyday language links it to a contemporary dramatic sub-genre of 'domestic tragedy'. Plays such as *The Yorkshire Tragedy* (attributed to Shakespeare when it was printed in 1608, and drawing on a true-crime story of wife-murder) or *Arden of Faversham* (anonymously published, but sometimes partly attributed to Shakespeare) typically deal with criminality, usually deriving from the wife's infidelity, amid the bourgeois classes. They are distinctively household in their location, but their themes resonate outside the simply domestic. Early modern ideas of order attempted to stabilize hierarchies by making them analogous: thus, the relation of servant to master or child to parent or wife to husband was equivalent to that of subject to sovereign. There was even a crime on the statute-book, petty treason, which captured this relationship: harsher punishments were due to aggravated forms of murder involving the killing of a superior by a subordinate: a husband by a wife, or a servant killing his master.

Lena Cowen Orlin summarizes domestic tragedy's usual analogical relation between household and state in which 'the mutual imprinting of domestic and political spheres [gave] the state cause to concern itself with order in all households and to enjoin good domestic governance as a public duty', and shows how these plays instate the household as 'a microcosm of the kingdom' (Orlin, 373). In *Macbeth* we can see the collapsing of this analogical model: the crime at the centre of the play is not the petty treason of murder of the head of the household, but the high treason of regicide, even as the king's presence in the domestic space ought to have invoked Macbeth's protection as 'kinsman' and 'host' (1.7.13–14). Amid the domestic detail of the scene's stage direction, Macbeth plots the murder of his sovereign. The jarring location of criminality within the material household clearly links *Macbeth* to adjacent domestic tragedies, which see Arden murdered at his backgammon table or Anne Sanders managing the fruit closet and linens of the household in *A Warning for Fair Women* (1599) while being persuaded to betray her husband. Perhaps the sequence at the beginning of Act 2 can stand for this domestic disruption:

> Go, bid thy mistress, when my drink is ready,
> She strike upon the bell. Get thee to bed. -
> Is this a dagger, which I see before me,
> The handle toward my hand? Come, let me clutch thee: -
> I have thee not, and yet I see thee still. (2.1.31–5)

In an instant, Macbeth switches from the apparently normal routine of bedtime – although the ringing of the bell is a signal in their murderous plan – to the high rhetorical drama of his hallucination. Domestic language and situations are wrested into new, strange shapes. It is no wonder that how the nameless Lord in 3.6 conceptualizes the defeat of Macbeth is in a return to domestic order: with the help of God and the English king, 'we may again/Give to our tables meat, sleep to our nights,/Free from our feasts and banquets bloody knives,/Do faithful homage' (3.6.33–6).

The witches

Related to this perversion of domesticity is the representation of the witches. Their supernatural, twilight world parodies and threatens that of the household. The First Witch is angered by the sailor's wife who will not share her chestnuts, and the Weird Sisters' actions twist gendered roles in the household even as the term used for them, 'sisters', seems to travesty familial relations. As Diane Purkiss notes in her study *The Witch in History*, the witches' cauldron with its grotesque ingredients: 'scale of dragon, tooth of wolf;/Witch's mummy; maw, and gulf,/Of the ravin'd salt-sea shark;/Root of hemlock, digg'd i'th'dark;/Liver of blaspheming Jew;/Gall of goat, and slips of yew' (4.1.22–7) is 'a recipe, albeit a parodic one; this becomes more tenable when we recall that books of housewifery were often composed in rhyme in the early modern period as an aide-memoire' (Purkiss, 212). And while the iconic power of the witches' scene means that cauldrons are now ineluctably associated with the supernatural, here the cauldron was an ordinary cooking utensil, like Lady Macbeth's blanket and knife, wrested to diabolic work. Shakespeare may have got the idea for this scene from the woodcut of women round a cauldron which illustrated the front of a pamphlet called *Newes from Scotland* (1591), a sensational account of witchcraft trials in Berwick in the early 1590s in which James VI of Scotland had interested himself. This publication about local small-town witchcraft provided some of the verbal details of Shakespeare's Weird Sisters. On the other hand, there are elements of the witches' presentation that come from a more elevated register and the scholarly discipline of demonology.

Visiting the University of Oxford in 1605, James was greeted by three sybils, classical figures of prophecy, who hailed him in Latin as ruler of a united Britain, and recalled the historical Banquo as his ancestor: it has been suggested, although there is no evidence to prove it, that Shakespeare might have been present or heard about this performance.

From the start, then, the Weird Sisters were ambivalent figures. Shakespeare seems to have used the second edition of Holinshed's *Chronicles* as his source here and for other historical plays, but had he consulted the first edition of 1577 he would have seen an illustration of three well-dressed courtly ladies, quite unlike the accompanying description of 'three women in strange & ferly apparel, resembling creatures of an elder world': text and image are contradictory. The presentation of the witches on the stage mirrors this juxtaposition of the mundane and the infernal, the everyday and the diabolic. Instructing the chorus of witches in his opera of the play, Verdi told them to be 'brutal and coarse' with each other but 'subtle and prophetic' in confronting Macbeth, and wrote his music to convey this shift (Kliman, 47). Sometimes the witches are spookily supernatural, as in the swirling mists of Orson Welles' opening sequence in his film of 1948, or the ghostly, androgynous figures painted by Henry Fuseli at the end of the eighteenth century. Max Stafford-Clark translated their speeches for his Out of Joint production (2004) to make them unsettlingly incomprehensible: the production notes explain that he 'had wanted to find a way of making the witches disturbing; they had ceased to be 'scary' in modern productions' (Out of Joint). But on other occasions the witches are represented more as misfit social victims than conduits to the devil. In Andrew Hilton's 2004 production in Bristol, for example, the witches 'look like ordinary village women. They have the resentment of those who have been poor too long', or, as another reviewer interpreted it, they 'are no mysterious of malevolent hags, but unusually young and comely, like adolescent girls dabbling in the black arts' (O'Connor, 743, 747). Linguistic choices, therefore, toggle between the mundane and the more elevated enact at a micro-level what the play stages more thematically and structurally.

Banquo's ghost

To conclude this section on domesticity in the play, we might cite the scene in which Banquo's ghost appears at the banquet as a particular example, dubbed by one reviewer with knowing bathos, 'the kind of dinner-party you would rather forget' (O'Connor, 680).

The scene, 3.4, opens with the stage direction 'Banquet prepar'd' (3.4.0SD): although the word 'banquet' is never spoken in the scene, its presence in the stage direction is a submerged echo or anticipation of Banquo's name (a pun anticipated by Duncan: 'True, worthy Banquo: he [Macbeth] is full so valiant,/And in his commendations I am fed;/It is a banquet to me' (1.4.54–6)). At the Macbeths' feast, repeated mention of Banquo's name calls him into horrific presence, 'were the grac'd person of our Banquo present' (3.4.40) and even as he attempts to recover himself from the shock of the ghost's appearance, Macbeth seems unable to resist toasting the murdered thane once more: 'I drink [. . .] to our dear friend Banquo, whom we miss' (3.4.88–9). This struck Simon Forman, an astrologer and doctor who saw the play performed at the Globe in 1611: the ghost appears just as 'he gain to speak of noble Banquo and to wish that he were there' (Brooke, 236). Emrys Jones identifies the 'schizophrenia' of the scene: 'Macbeth's genuine desire for Banquo to be present coupled with his fear lest he should' is part of the 'divided motivation' of the plot (Jones, 214). For the first time, this stage direction marks Macbeth's entrance 'as King'. Macbeth welcomes his guests and invites them to 'drink a measure' (3.4.11). Into this scene of conviviality enters the murderer, with 'blood upon thy face' (3.4.13): Macbeth's world, the position from which he greets the lords, is quite literally blood-stained. And there is more blood to come. The next figure to enter is 'the Ghost of Banquo, and sits in Macbeths place' (3.4.40SD). This was the scene most recalled by Forman, who had a keen eye for its particular choreography:

> being at supper with his nobleman whom he had bid to a feast, to the which also Banquo should have come, he began to speak of noble Banquo, and to wish that he were there. And as he thus did, standing up to drink a carouse to him, the ghost of Banquo came and sat down in his chair behind him; and he, turning about to sit down again, saw the ghost of Banquo, which fronted him so, that he fell into a great passion of fear and fury. (Brooke, 236)

Banquo's ghost has 'gory locks' (3.4.50) and the air of the vacated 'charnel house' (3.4.70). Lady Macbeth's attempts to cover the confusion and embarrassment again try to belittle Macbeth with bathetic comparisons: 'these flaws and starts,/ (Imposters to true fear), would well become/A woman's story at a winter's fire,/Authorized by her grandam. Shame itself!' (3.4.62–5). Macbeth excuses his 'strange infirmity' (3.4.85) and attempts again to resume the toast. Our feeling, notes Emrys Jones in a finely appropriate paradox, is 'tragic embarrassment': 'tragedy' and 'embarrassment' seem to be different orders of experience but here they are juxtaposed (Jones, 217).

When the ghost returns, Macbeth's language is epic:

Approach thou like the rugged Russian bear,
The arm'd rhinoceros, or th'Hyrcan tiger;
Take any shape but that. (3.4.99–101)

When the ghost departs his diction returns to something more everyday: 'why, so: – being gone,/I am a man again' (3.4.106–7). The juxtaposition of registers is stark, as is the deployment of perspective: the stage direction indicates that Banquo's ghost does indeed appear, and that he is unseen by everyone on stage but Macbeth.

At this point in the play, then, our view of the world is precisely aligned with that of Macbeth himself, and we are alienated from the other characters who do not see a figure who is plainly visible to us. In Max Stafford-Clark's production of 2004 the audience was invited to sit at the table and participate at close range with the horrifying events. Stafford-Clark used a promenade-style production and an African setting to disrupt audience comfort and to bring out the play's political violence: 'In a traditional auditorium there is a contract between the actor and the audience; accepted barriers define the ownership of the space.' Stafford-Clark wanted to transcend that contract and make it more uncomfortable, 'in the same way as those news pictures are uncomfortable for us' (Out of Joint).

The language of the scene manipulates the extraordinary – the irruption of the dead man – with the usual – the scene of the banquet. In Adrian Noble's 1986 production, Macbeth pulled the table-cloth from the table in lunging at the ghost, then tried to smooth it out. Harriet Walter recalls: 'It was so banal, that gesture of setting the table again! That's what I liked about our production. Again and again we were allowed as actors to not be those huge tragic figures but sometimes to be terribly domestic, terribly mundane, so that it brought the level of that evil into an area we all know' (Walter, 69).

The scene with Banquo's ghost stages the consequences of Macbeth's crimes in the heart of the household, at a banquet intended to unify the lords in celebration of their new king. Macbeth's language elides Banquo and Duncan as his victims:

> the time has been,
> That, when the brains were out, the man would die,
> And there an end; but now they rise again,
> With twenty mortal murthers on their crowns,
> And push us from our stools. (3.4.77–81)

The 'stools' here are usually glossed by editors as 'thrones' but it is in keeping with the scene's flirtation with bathos that they are simple backless seats. The 'crowns' here are both the crown of the head: the murderer reports that Banquo has 'twenty trenched gashes on his head' (3.4.26). But they are also the royal crown: Macbeth, in killing a king, has murders on his crown too, and even in death Banquo pushes him from his usurped throne, which is only ever a stool.

The juxtaposition of banal and momentous continues to the end of the scene. While Macbeth vows 'to the Weird sisters [. . .] for now I am bent to know,/By the worst means, the worst' (3.4.132–4), Lady Macbeth urges sleep, 'the season of all natures' (3.4.140). Harriet Walter recalls how this line developed as she and Antony Sher rehearsed the scene:

> Then one rehearsal, Tony looked at me and I looked at him and the lameness and absurdity of that one and the agony and horror of what we had done and what we had become burst spontaneously out of both of us with a terrible giggling laughter. We managed to recreate that moment every night. It was the last flash of togetherness before Macbeth leaves the room to wade deeper into crime and to be become better at it . . . we would not meet onstage again. (Walter, 53)

Sher and Walter's hysterical laughter indicates how the jumpiness of this scene comes close to a kind of black humour. Perhaps because of this, the scene of Banquo's ghost appears to have been parodied by contemporary plays including Middleton's *The Puritan* (1606) and Beaumont's *The Knight of the Burning Pestle* (1607). In the Middleton play, a character invites others to a 'banquet' where 'we'll ha' the ghost i'th' white sheet sit at the upper end o'th'table'. In Beaumont's parody of chivalric romance, performed within a year or so of *Macbeth*, Jasper pretends to be a ghost with his face 'mealed' (whitened with flour):

> never shalt thou sit or be alone
> In any place but I will visit thee

With ghastly looks, and put into thy mind
The great offences which thou didst to me.
When thou art at thy table with thy friends,
Merry in heart, and filled with swelling wine,
I'll come in midst of all thy pride and mirth,
Invisible to all men but thyself,
And whisper such a sad tale in thine ear
Shall make thee let the cup fall from thy hand
And stand as mute and pale as Death itself.

The image of the mute, pale-faced ghost appearing at the table but visible only to the guilty man gives us a clear reminder of Banquo's entrance in *Macbeth*. If the cup falling from the petrified hand gives us a clue about the way the scene was originally performed, it is a piece of stage business which has lasted: Olivier and Finch are among the modern Macbeths who have dropped their goblet in shock at the appearance. Simon Forman was not the only viewer to be captivated by this particular episode in the play. It has been one of the locations for specific directorial intervention. In Orson Welles' film of 1948, for example, the film shifts from shots of a crowded banquet table to shots of one deserted except for a ghost. Welles has the ghost represent different characters at its two entrances: first Banquo, and next Duncan. The first half of Michael Boyd's Royal Shakespeare Company production of 2010 ended with a version of the banquet scene in which Banquo slit Macbeth's throat: showing the audience the 'nightmarish fantasies', as one reviewer put it, of its guilt-ridden hero. The second half opened with the same scene, replayed without Banquo present: Macbeth's agonies in this version have no visible cause, and our distance from him caused uneasy laughter in parts of the audience.

Review

This chapter has introduced the textual issues around *Macbeth* and clarified some of the choices different editors make about how to present the words in front of us. Then it has focused on the ways that verbal detail builds up dramatic effects, emphasizing specific words and their network of associations across the play. In analysing Macbeth's soliloquy in 1.7, we have introduced techniques to focus attention on lexicon and rhythm, and the ways in which form and content are mutually reinforcing. In discussing *Macbeth*'s everyday language as part of the genre of 'domestic tragedy', we have begun to see how specific words and clusters of imagery can be aggregated to understand tone and theme in the play as a whole.

Writing matters

I Analysing the speech

Review the techniques deployed above to consider Macbeth's soliloquy: thinking about the language choice, the rhythm and the punctuation; reading down the right hand margin for the flow of thoughts; working out where stresses might fall in verse lines; using a concordance or searchable online text to trace repeated words; consulting a digital version of the Folio online to look at matters of punctuation, lineation and capitalization and how your editor has dealt with them. Remember to think about the speech in the context of the play: what's just happened, and what will happen next? How does this moment of contemplation fit into an onward narrative?

Now, try to practise these by applying them either to Macbeth's speech at the end of 4.1 (beginning 'Time, thou anticipat'st my dread exploits') or 3.1.46 – ('To be thus is nothing'). Your task is to recognize, and write about, the poetic density and the emotional complexity of the chosen speech, rather than to try to paraphrase it into more readily understood language. Have the confidence to identify words as complex or unusual, or syntax as knotty and confused or thoughts as complex or incomplete. Use an online complete works to check your instincts about what words are rare; look online and compare your edition with the speech as it looks in the Folio text. Rhetorical devices or figures of speech were well-known to early modern writers and used consciously to ornament their composition: you might want to look up in a dictionary the most common devices or start with the ones below, and begin to develop this specialist vocabulary in your own analysis and writing.

II Rhetorical terms

Anaphora: Repetition of the same word(s) at the beginning of successive lines

> All hail, Macbeth! hail to thee, Thane of Glamis!
> All hail, Macbeth! hail to thee, Thane of Cawdor!
> All hail, Macbeth! that shalt be King hereafter. (1.3.48–50)

Apostrophe: Highly charged or emotional comment

> O horror! horror! horror! (2.3.63)

Asyndeton: Omission of conjunctions

> As hounds, and greyhounds, mongrels, spaniels, curs,
> Shoughs, water-rugs, and demi-wolves, are clept
> All by the name of dogs: the valu'd file
> Distinguishes the swift, the slow, the subtle,
> The housekeeper, the hunter. (3.1.92–6)

Chiasmus: Parallel ideas or words repeated in an inverted pattern (ABBA)

> Fair is foul and foul is fair. (1.1.11)

Epanalepsis: Repetition of the beginning word/s at the end of a phrase or sentence

It will have blood, they say: blood will have blood. (3.4.121)

Hyperbole: Exaggeration for emphasis

Will all great Neptune's ocean wash this blood
Clean from my hand? (2.2.59–60)

Isocolon: Phrases of equal length and comparable structure

it makes him and it mars him; it sets him on and it takes
him off; it persuades him, and disheartens him; makes him
stand to, and not stand to. (2.4.32–5)

Paranomasia: Repetition of the same word in different form

If it were done when 'tis done, 'twere well it were done
quickly. (1.7.1)

Ploce: Repetition of the same word, sometimes after the intervention of one or two other words

'Sleep no more!
Macbeth does murther Sleep' – the innocent Sleep
Sleep, the knits up the ravell'd sleeve of care. (2.2.34–6)

Metonymy: substitution of the part for the whole

All that doth impede thee from the golden round (where
'round' is the crown, a metonym for kingship). (1.5.27)

III *Searching for particular words*

Use an online text to search for words with the prefix 'over' or
'un'. Some of the ones you might find are overtake, overcome,
overthrown, overcharged, overcredulous, overred; unseamed,
unsex, unspeak, unwiped, unbattered, undeeded, unbend,
unbecoming, unlined. Look up these words in a concordance
to see whether and where they appear in other plays, and focus
in particular on those which are unique to *Macbeth* or rarely
found elsewhere. How might these two kinds of words – one
indicating excess or surplus, the other indicating negation – fit
in with the wider themes of the play? How do they contribute
to its atmosphere and structure?

CHAPTER TWO

Language and structure

In Chapter One the focus was on the techniques of close analysis of individual speeches, building up to an understanding of how the play's poetry serves to draw together its themes. Here in Chapter Two the focus is on how the language of *Macbeth* is devised to structure the play, to unfold the plot through stage-time and to develop its themes. We will look closely at Shakespeare's construction of his plot and his emphasis compared to the stories that he found in his source material. The final section considers the emphasis on time, temporality and the notion of the future in the play.

Construction

Macbeth is divided into five acts – a classical structure that Shakespeare would have observed in the Roman plays of Terence and Seneca, but one which appears consistently only in play-texts prepared for the indoor theatre of Blackfriars (after 1609). The four act breaks in a five-act play allowed for the candles that lit the stage to be trimmed and replaced (given the risk of fire in timber-framed building, this maintenance was crucial). The five acts of *Macbeth* are marked in the Folio text (thus suggesting the text dates from a period later than the 1606 date usually given for the play), but in fact, the play more naturally divides itself into three.

Three movements attach themselves to different antagonists (Jones). In the first section of the play, Macbeth's antagonist – or so he convinces himself – is Duncan: the narrative here is about the preparation and execution of Duncan's murder, and lasts until the end of Act 2. The threat in the next section comes from Banquo, and the scenes depict the plan to kill him, the bungled ambush and the entry of the ghost to the banquet – ending in 3.4. Only in the final third, ushered in by Macbeth's second visit to the witches, does the threat from Macduff and Malcolm materialize, gather strength and overwhelm the usurping king in his castle. James Agate noted some of the difficulties caused by the effective evacuation of Macbeth's role in the final two acts:

> With the banqueting scene, which is only half-way, the part is almost over. After that we have the apparition scene in which Macbeth is virtually a spectator. Then comes the murder of Lady Macduff, the long business about Malcolm, the revelation to Macduff, and the sleep-walking scene. Macbeth's next appearance is with Seyton, and whether the play is to stand or fall depends upon the power of the actor to suggest the ravages of mind, soul, and even body endured since we saw him last. (Braunmuller, 27)

One further consequence of this structure is that Malcolm, as Macbeth's ultimate successor, is virtually silenced until the final movement of the play, and Macduff, too, is a nemesis whose introduction to the action is decidedly belated. The scene in Act 2 when he is knocking at the door of the castle emphasizes his tardy entrance into the play, arriving when its most important action is already completed: 'Wake Duncan with thy knocking: I would thou couldst' (2.2.73).

This triadic structure is, of course, intrinsic to concepts of storytelling at their most basic, corresponding to the beginning, middle and end division of classical narrative, sometimes divided into 'set-up', 'confrontation' and 'resolution', or 'exposition', 'rising action' and 'climax'. But it has a more specific effect here. The structure of the play serves to place the emphasis on Macbeth throughout, and its three movements correspond with the play's own repeated evocations of the structure of three, embodied most obviously in the three Weird Sisters and their opening chant 'when shall we three meet again?' (1.1.1). The play's first movement involves Macbeth acting on the suggestion that he will become king; in the second he is preoccupied with the implications of their predictions to Banquo. The play's final section takes up their second prophecies about Birnam Wood, no man born of woman, and the dangerous Macduff. As we shall see in this section, the language and stagecraft used to structure the play emphasizes its speed and its moral ambiguity.

Structure

Macbeth is one of Shakespeare's shortest plays: at 2,500 lines it is a full hour shorter than *Hamlet* (that hero is still in his mother's chamber at the equivalent point when Macbeth's head is brought in to the valiant king) or *Henry V* (still in the midst of the battle of Agincourt) or *Romeo and Juliet* (Juliet is just drinking the sleeping draught as *Macbeth* finishes). One of the predominant impressions of the play is thus that of speed. The play's decisive act, the murder of King Duncan, happens with a rapidity that is extraordinary. Almost every scene is compressed, compacted, moving with a remorseless energy that will not allow a backward look or hesitation. Those that are not stand out: Macbeth's unexpectedly loquacious encounter with the murderers as he commissions Banquo's assassination, for instance, or the strangely distended scene in which Malcolm tests Macduff's loyalty.

This play has no time for a sub-plot, no parallel or contrasting group of characters. With great structural economy, it doesn't even bother to introduce characters until needed – Macduff, for instance – and dispatches them without ceremony when they have served their purpose – the 'bloody' captain, for example, who is so important to the play's opening and never heard of again, or the murderers, or even Duncan himself, who, once he has been established as the saintly ruler whose death sets nature into turmoil, is hardly spoken of again in the entire play. It rushes pell-mell from its first word, which is, appropriately, a question of time and of futurity: 'when shall we three meet again?' (1.1.1). Even Malcolm's final speech emphasizes a rush to confirm the military victory with political settlement: 'We shall not spend a large expense of time/ Before we reckon with your several loves,/ And make us even with you' (5.9.26–7).

Although *Macbeth* is not uniquely short – *The Comedy of Errors* and *The Tempest* are both shorter – it has nevertheless been suggested that the play as we have it is abbreviated. John Dover Wilson, editing the play in 1947 for the landmark Cambridge series, proposed that Shakespeare had abridged the play and that a number of scenes could be conjectured as missing. Dover Wilson imagines a 'larger dramatic frame' in which Macbeth meets his wife to convey his encounter with the Weird Sisters, and suggests that Lady Macbeth's 'my keen knife' indicates that she means to undertake the murder herself and that the unexplained change of dramatic plan is due to revision or abridgement (Dover Wilson, xxxvi). He feels that the placing of Duncan's murder is pre-emptory and should properly belong to Act 3, and attributes long-standing mysteries about the play such as the identity of the third murderer to the compression of an originally longer play.

There is no external evidence to suggest that the play has been cut. And while writing scenes Shakespeare didn't is fun (Macduff's farewell to his family? Malcolm's discussions with the English king? Lady Macbeth's views on her husband's increasing emotional distance?), often the attempt to do it tells us something of why the experienced playwright chose not to. We could meet Dover Wilson's concerns about the plotting of *Macbeth* with the claim of dramaturgical effectiveness. The play works well as we have it: that there is no scene in which the Macbeths explicitly plan that the response to the witches' prediction is to murder Duncan is less something missing than it is an economical way to tell us about their intuitive mental intimacy, for example. Gaps in the play narrative are crucial spaces for the reader or director imaginatively to occupy: they are interpretative vents in the drama. The evasions and ellipses of the plot enact on a structural level those verbal elisions that compress the play's language into its characteristically compact form: 'if 'twere done when 'tis done' (1.7.1).

Showing and telling

The structure of the play thus frequently forces us to experience the haste that is intrinsic to its plot. And in its management of the dramatic arts of showing – *mimesis* – and telling – *diegesis* – the play enacts its own curious, and appropriate, coarsening. The murder of Duncan is described, not shown, in the play (although film versions find it irresistible, such as Polanski's, in which a naked sleeping Duncan wakes to gasp 'Macbeth!' as the loyal thane kills him). Like Macbeth himself in 1.7 (see Chapter One), that's to say, the play finds it difficult to face this terrible deed. In describing rather than visualizing it, the play enacts in its oblique representational terms the kind of verbal euphemism of 'deed' and 'taking-off' that we noted in Macbeth's soliloquy (1.7.14, 20). This is not some general cultural squeamishness about presenting the murder of a king onstage: Shakespeare had done that without qualms in *Richard II*, for instance. Rather, it is part of a pattern of withholding visual material, managing audience sympathies and pacing the play.

We can see the effects of this by comparing the offstage murder of Duncan with the scene in which Macbeth's brutes arrive at Macduff's castle. By the time Lady Macduff's children are being slaughtered at their castle in Fife, the play has lost its scruples about the representation of violence. We are all of us – the audience as well as Macbeth himself – in 'blood/ Stepp'd in so far' (3.4.135–6), that this horrific scene has to be visualized, interpolated to try to revive our brutalized theatrical appetites. Or, perhaps, in the scene as Polanski gives us it, complete with the strong implication of rape and murder, further to brutalize us. Max Stafford-Clark's disturbing production of 2004 made clear the queasy position of the spectators of such brutality: armed soldiers encouraged the promenade audience to pay to enter a small room to see the bloody corpses for themselves. The question of why tragedy gives us pleasure is a thorny one, but one that is inescapable when part of that 'pleasure' is looking on while acts of savagery take place. The murder of Macduff's 'wife, children, servants, all/ That could be found' (4.3.210–11) is a uniquely, and perhaps gratuitously, sadistic piece of theatre: nowhere else in Shakespeare are characters introduced and humanized for the sole purpose of being put to death for our gratification.

Like Macbeth, then, we are in danger of being anaesthetized against violence. We have already experienced the murders of a king and his grooms and of Banquo, the appearance of his 'blood-bolter'd' ghost (4.1.123) and the bloody child of the witches' apparitions. With the Macduff murders, the play tries to wake up our outrage as part of its shift towards the new order of Malcolm's reign. It is followed immediately by the scene between Malcolm and Macduff, then that of the doctor and the gentlewoman observing Lady Macbeth's sleepwalking, then the scene with the thanes leading their soldiers towards Dunsinane. Thus, it is one of the means by which the play changes gear, aligning itself with Macbeth's victims rather than, as before, with his own tortured psyche. Macbeth is now offstage for four consecutive scenes, having hitherto missed only four in total since his first entrance: the balance of interest has shifted towards his antagonists. Malcolm, who has spoken only 30 or so lines in the whole play, now has a scene with 142 – more than two-thirds of his total part. And Lady Macbeth's sleepwalking scene, with its haunted, obsessive reliving of the night of Duncan's murder, serves to recap the plot of the play in preparation for its final resolution. That her own death is reported, not shown, and that it prompts so little response in her husband, is a symptom of the play's burnt-out representation, retreating from mimesis back to diegesis, weary of events just as Macbeth himself is weary of life as 'a poor player,/ That struts and frets his hour upon the stage,/ And then is heard no more' (5.5.24–6).

Leaving certain scenes to the imagination is thus important in creating and sustaining audience response. When we see the death speech that the eighteenth-century Shakespearean actor David Garrick wrote for the hero's final breath – 'Tis done! the scene of life will quickly close. Ambition's vain delusive dreams are fled. And now I wake to darkness, guilt, and horror; I cannot bear it! let me shake it off – it will not be; my soul is clog'd with blood – I cannot rise! I dare not ask for mercy – It is too late, hell drags me down; I sink, I sink, – my soul is lost for ever! – oh! – oh!' (Furness, 295) – we may well feel relieved that Shakespeare let Macbeth die with his last words of defiance as he and Macduff engage in single combat: 'lay on, Macduff;/ And damn'd be him that first cries, "Hold, enough!"' (5.8.33–4). Garrick's speech, heavily influenced by Dr Faustus's realization of his eternal damnation at the end of Marlowe's play, is too declarative, too straightforward, just too clear, for Shakespeare, who leaves Macbeth's understanding of his situation as only ever implicit.

Terror and horror

The play's characteristic juxtaposition between representational clarity and obscurity, or between mimesis and diegesis, or between statement and suggestion, is at the heart of a discussion of the difference between 'terror' and 'horror' which has been an influential critical axis in discussions of Gothic fiction and the literary representation of fear. Ann Radcliffe, well-known as the author of seminal Gothic novels including *The Mysteries of Udolfo* (1794) and *The Italian* (1796), wrote 'On the Supernatural in Poetry', a dialogue between two companions reflecting on the literary taste for fearsome tales. Horror is agreed to be the more vulgar literary effect, whereas terror approaches the sublime, the highest accolade in eighteenth-century aesthetics. The entrance of Banquo to Macbeth's feast is given as an example of horror, rather than terror: terror, for Mrs. Radcliffe, is the more powerful since it is the reader's own response to uncertainty, obscurity and indirect representation. What is imagined is always more terrible than what is directly shown. Banquo's entrance provokes an impression that while it is 'sudden and strong, is also transient; it is the thrill of horror and surprise'; true terror is 'gloomy and sublime' (Radcliffe). It is a version of Macbeth's own early recognition that 'present fears/ Are less than horrible imaginings' (1.3.137–8).

Seeing *Macbeth*, as Radcliffe does, as a version of gothic fiction throws up some revealing insights. An internet advice guide to would-be horror film screenwriters is a useful parallel to the dramaturgy here, and brings out some of the structural echoes between *Macbeth* and other stories of the struggle between good and evil typical of the horror genre:

1   The hook. Start with a bang. (Unlike other Shakespeare plays which start with a sideways look at the main action, often from inconsequential characters, *Macbeth* begins with just such a suspense scene from the witches.)

2   The flaw. Introduce your hero. Give him a flaw. Before you can put your hero in jeopardy we must care for him. (Shakespeare's use of asides in 1.4 and soliloquy in 1.7 makes us enter into a special relationship with Macbeth.)

3   No escape. Have your hero at an isolated location where he can't escape the horror. (Shakespeare adheres to this convention, too, although the isolated location is a psychological one: Macbeth cannot escape himself.)

4 Foreplay. Tease the audience. Give them some more foreplay before bringing in the real monster. (Not exactly foreplay, but the scenes of suspense around Duncan's murder might function in a similar way.)

5 Evil attacks. A couple of times during the middle of the script show how evil the monster can be as it attacks its victims. (The scenes of the attack on Banquo and Fleance, and on the Macduff household, serve this function, but most importantly, but what we see is the terrifying conflation in Shakespeare's drama of the role of hero and monster: Macbeth plays both.)

6 Showdown. The final confrontation. The hero has to face both his fear and the monster. (Macbeth and Macduff fight together: Macbeth seems to be fighting a version of himself and his own demons.)

7 Aftermath. Everything's back to the way it was from the beginning – but the hero has changed for the better or for the worse. (Malcolm's accession to the throne can be either a sign of growth and regeneration – the natural imagery associated with Duncan makes a return to the play's language – or of repetition: one stage version visualized the clothing imagery – see Chapter Three – in its final image of Malcolm trying on a leather greatcoat dropped by Macbeth. The implication was that nothing had changed.)

8 Evil lurks. We see evidence that the monster may return somewhere . . . somehow . . . in the future. (Interestingly, there is no closing scene with the witches, although film versions tend to import one. In Welles' film it is the quietist 'Peace! – the charm's wound up' (1.3.37): his witches acknowledge the establishment of a rightful king as the completion of their plot and, implicitly, the end of their active role in the playworld. In Polanski's it is quite different: a mutinous-looking Donalbain escapes from the

celebrations of Malcolm's coronation and appears
to follow the same route that took Macbeth and
Banquo to the witches. Like them, he hears a strange
singing; like them, he dismounts to investigate. The
implication is that the whole cycle might begin again.
An alternative ending might stress Fleance and the yet
unfulfilled prophecy.)

The structure and implication of the play's conclusion forms
part of its ethical ambiguity. Macbeth's head on a pole recalls
that of the earlier traitor Macdonwald, 'fix'd . . . upon our battlements' (1.2.23), just as the triple 'hail' (5.9.20–5) acknowledging Malcolm's right echoes the witches' prophecies. As
Harry Berger points out, this could be read as poetic justice –
the wheel has come full circle – or existential repetition – there
is only more of the same to come. The different cinematic interpretations of the witches at the end of the films by Welles and
Polanski do something similar: suggesting closure in the first
and endless repetition in the second. Like Macbeth, Macduff
has killed a crowned king: the structural similarity of the two
regicides is in tension with their apparent moral differentiation.
And the ending of the play is shaped by the way we interpret the
representation of Malcolm as the new king.

The role of Malcolm

Part of the problem about Malcolm as the great ideological
hope of the play is that he is such a non-entity. In *Richard III*,
another play about usurpation (see Introduction), Shakespeare
withholds the introduction of Richard's nemesis Richmond
until the very end of the play: he emerges as something akin to
the *deus ex machina* figure of classical drama, an uncharac-
terized force whose sole function is to bring the play to a conclusion. The presentation of Malcolm is not quite the same.
First, Malcolm does not seem to play a very active role in
Scotland's wars at the play's opening. Further, nobody reacts

when Duncan announces: 'We will establish our estate upon/ Our eldest, Malcolm; whom we name hereafter/ The Prince of Cumberland' (1.4.37–9): it is not a signal for rejoicing or congratulation among the seven other people onstage. Perhaps this is related to the fact that there is no immediate acclamation of Malcolm's succession when Duncan's death is discovered. Nor is it entirely clear why Malcolm and Donalbain chose to flee Scotland – and even if it seems humanly sensible to get as far away as possible, it isn't exactly heroic to run from the scene of your father's murder. Jacobean playgoers, brought up on revenge tragedies powered by the bloody retribution exacted for a family death, would have been distinctly unimpressed. So far, so flat.

And the majority of Malcolm's lines in the play come in a strange scene that tests Macduff's loyalty even as it strains the play's structure. Malcolm and Macduff's discussion in England is an odd moment in the play. Both these characters are rather opaque to us at this point, as a numerical snapshot reveals. Malcolm has been present in four scenes in one of which (1.6) he was silent: so far he has spoken around 30 lines in the play. Macduff has been present in three scenes and was also silent in one of these, giving him a total of around 55 lines so far. Neither, then, is particularly familiar to the audience, so we are alert for clues. Malcolm opens by inviting Macduff 'Let us seek out some desolate shade, and their/Weep our sad bosoms empty' (4.3.1–2). Macduff is having none of this passive wailing: 'Let us rather/ Hold fast the mortal sword' (4.3.2–3). Malcolm imagines himself betrayed by Macduff in terms that aspire to a kind of Christlike self-sacrifice (productions of the play often have Malcolm costumed here as a monkishly religious figure): 'a weak, poor, innocent lamb,/ T'appease an angry god' (4.3.16–7). This is not the language of muscular moral or physical opposition to Macbeth's tyranny. As the scene unfolds, the tone is distinctly off-key. We have just seen Macduff's family exterminated, left unprotected and 'fatherless' (4.2.26). Malcolm's question 'Why in that rawness left you wife and child'? (4.3.26) remains unanswered and unanswerable, echoing Lady Macduff's 'He loves us not:/ He wants the natural touch' (4.2.8–9), and thus serves rather to undermine Macduff than to elevate him as the ethical alternative to Macbeth.

If Macduff's character is overshadowed by the accusation he has abandoned his family, then Malcolm's character too is muddied: his longest speeches in the scene construct a narrative of himself as avaricious, lustful and lacking all 'the king-becoming graces' he lists as 'Justice, Verity, Temp'rance, Stableness/ Bounty, Perseverance, Mercy, Lowliness,/ Devotion, Patience, Courage, Fortitude' (4.3.91–4). This catalogue reveals that one of the functions of the scene must relate to contemporary political debates. We see the play debating different notions of kingship and the relative importance of might and right. Here the discussion is about fitness to rule. Malcolm establishes himself as a fit king as well as, by Duncan's election, the rightful king. The scene emphasizes the personal attributes of the ruler as crucial to his success. This may seem uncontentious but, of course, in a hereditary system it is potentially dynamite – bringing two potentially discrepant systems of evaluation into conjunction. The question of who might be a good king is unaskable in a context where kingship is passed on through birth not merit. But what is also difficult about the scene is that Malcolm spends so large a proportion of his relatively small part in the play perjuring himself. The purpose of this self-slander is to test Macduff's loyalty, and the thane survives the test. Having attempted to reconcile Malcolm's confession – 'we have willing dames enough' (4.3.73); 'Scotland hath foisons to fill up your will' (4.3.88) – Macduff explodes in a desolate apostrophe: 'O Scotland! Scotland! . . . Fit to govern? / No, not to live' (4.3.100–3).

But there is something a little adrift about the balance of the scene, perhaps – since there is not quite time for Malcolm fully to dispel the image of himself he has created:

> I am yet
> Unknown to woman; never was forsworn;

Scarcely have coveted what was mine own,
At no time broke my faith: would not betray
The Devil to his fellow; and delight
No less in truth, than life. (4.3.125–30)

The play is not structured to allow Macduff to take this in.
His response bespeaks bewilderment: 'Such welcome and
unwelcome things at once/ Tis hard to reconcile' (4.3.138–9),
and then the scene moves on to another image of moral kingship. The 'good King' of England heals the sick by 'Hanging
a golden stamp about their necks/ Put on with holy prayers'
(4.3.147, 153–4): he never appears in the play (sometimes
productions interpolate a kind of holy tableau depicting him)
and his only purpose here seems to be to amplify an otherwise rather abstract political discussion about the nature of
a good ruler.

We can pick up some of these implications looking at a
modern adaptation of *Macbeth*. Something of the existential
emptiness of Macbeth's own recognition that life is 'a tale/
Told by an idiot, full of sound and fury/ Signifying nothing'
(5.5.26–8), made the play a particular influence on European
absurdist theatre in the twentieth century. Two reworkings
stand out in particular. Alfred Jarry's controversial 1896 play
Ubu Roi parodied the play with a plotline involving Pere
Ubu, a man persuaded by his wife Mere Ubu, to murder the
king. The play's poetry is replaced by a scatalogical dialogue
that lays bare its animalistic impulses. The second, Eugene
Ionesco's *Macbett* (1972) also develops a farcical take on
the play's brutality, turning it into a Cold War allegory of
political absurdism. Ionesco's adaptation collapses any sense
of moral distinction between the characters. At the end of
Ionesco's play, Macol, the Malcolm figure (although he is the
son of Banquo rather than Duncan) defeats Macbett, and,
with the crown, assumes Macbett's tyranny also. It is at this
point – when he is being hailed as king – that Macol delivers
what in Shakespeare's 4.3 is Malcolm's mis-representation of
himself as unprincipled, but here without any ironic subtext.

King Macol confesses himself depraved: the proposed deliverance from tyranny is a false dawn. The plot is circular because ambition and the lust for power are not comfortingly identified as the aberrant property of an individual – as Shakespeare partly represents it. In Ionesco, as in Polanski, they are an unending chain, but whereas Polanski sees the next cycle of wickedness located in the opaque figure of the younger brother Donalbain, Ionesco draws out the ambiguities implicit in Shakespeare's presentation of Malcolm himself.

Shakespeare at work: Holinshed's *Chronicles*

The how-to guide to horror-writing cited above suggests how a modern writer might tailor a screenplay to a proven formula. Originality in this context depends on how skilfully you deploy the conventions, rather than on an ability to rewrite the rulebook. Something similar could be said for the early modern theatre and for Shakespeare's use of existing genres and plotlines. Shakespeare rarely completely innovates either in plot or in form, and *Macbeth*'s unique power is built on some pre-existing dramatic and historical foundations.

We know tantalizingly little about Shakespeare's working habits. Generations of biographers have been frustrated by the absence of any real evidence about Shakespeare the artist, particularly since we do know some things about Shakespeare the property-owner and Shakespeare the actor. The extant documents about Shakespeare's life, as for most early modern individuals, are financial and legal, not personal. It is not true to say, though, as those who seek to place Shakespeare's authorship of the plays in question, that there is something mysterious about the absence of early modern records: scholars fossicking in archives have found more material relating to Shakespeare than just about any other contemporary writer. But it is true that there are no manuscript drafts (we have only a handful of the hundreds of early modern plays that were written and performed now surviving in manuscript) and that no descriptive material about Shakespeare's own aims exists. Unlike his contemporary Ben Jonson, Shakespeare did not write prologues in which he set out his aesthetic philosophy; after the publication of his narrative poems *Venus and Adonis* and *The Rape of Lucrece* in the early 1590s he did not address himself to any patron; traces of his own personality often seem to be completely subsumed by the individual liveliness of all his dramatic protagonists. The image of Shakespeare on the psychiatrist's couch and unable to write which opens John Madden's film *Shakespeare in Love* (1998) is attractive – it cuts Shakespeare down to size, making him the author of a clearly flawed play labouring under the title 'Romeo and Ethel the pirate's daughter' – but probably inaccurate. Shakespeare wrote almost 40 plays comprising almost a million words over a writing career of about two decades: writer's block was not his problem.

When Shakespeare's contemporaries praised him it was for his verbal facility: Francis Meres called him 'honey-tongued', and Ben Jonson's recollection of his rival suggested that this characteristic linguistic ease needed more discipline:

> I remember the players have often mentioned it as an honour to Shakespeare, that in his writing, whatsoever he penned, he never blotted out line. My answer hath been, 'Would he had blotted a thousand'; which they thought a malevolent speech. I had not told posterity this but for their ignorance, who choose that circumstance to commend their friend by wherein he most faulted; and to justify mine own candour: for I loved the man, and do honour his memory, on this side idolatry, as much as any. He was, indeed, honest, and of an open and free nature; had an excellent fantasy, brave notions and gentle expressions; wherein he flowed with that facility that sometimes it was necessary he should be stopped. '*Sufflaminandus erat*' [sometimes he needed the brake], as Augustus said of Haterius. His wit was in his

own power; would the rule of it had been so too. Many times he fell into those things, could not escape laughter: as when he said in the person of Caesar, one speaking to him, 'Caesar, thou dost me wrong'; he replied, 'Caesar did never wrong, but with just cause'; and such like: which were ridiculous. But he redeemed his vices with his virtues. There was ever more in him to be praised than to be pardoned. (Jonson, 539–40)

It was the actor–editors of the First Folio who suggested that Shakespeare never blotted a line as he wrote. In their preface to the 1623 volume, entitled 'To the great variety of readers', John Heminge and Henry Condell claimed that the texts they published were the perfect exemplars of Shakespeare's art: 'Who, as he was a happy imitator of nature, was a most gentle expresser of it. His mind and hand went together, and what he thought, he uttered with that easiness, that we have scarce received from him a blot in his papers'.

The idea of the genius Shakespeare whose works sprang fully formed from his creative brain is a myth (and dispelling it does not reduce Shakespeare's achievement; rather, it shows the hard work behind it). More recent scholarship on Shakespeare has recognized that Heminge and Condell give us less an account of Shakespeare's working methods and more a sales pitch – half of the plays in this collected volume had already been on sale in London's bookstalls, so it was in the commercial interests of the editors to disparage those earlier versions and present their own book as the ultimate version. Think of the marketing of books or DVD films now: 'Director's cut', 'fully restored', 'digitally remastered', '20th anniversary edition': we can see that these are often attempts to make us buy a product that is substantially the same as one we already own, by suggesting that the previous copy is outdated or deficient in some crucial way. Further, we now know that Shakespeare did rework his own plays, revising words, lines and scenes. The two texts of *King Lear* are examples of this process of revision, and studying a parallel version of the editions printed in 1608 and in 1623 can give us some insight into Shakespeare at work, adding and cutting material to reshape the story, as well as tinkering with minor details ('the division of the kingdom' versus 'the division of the kingdoms' (1.1.4), for instance, where the singular is the 1623 reading and the plural from 1608).

No such textual variation exists with *Macbeth*, however, because the play only exists in one early modern version, the Folio of 1623 (as discussed in Chapter One). The Introduction suggested some of the ways this play draws on the other tragedies and on plays about regime change written earlier in Shakespeare's career. But the closest we can get in *Macbeth* to seeing Shakespeare's writing practices is by comparing his play with its source: the history of Scotland as published as part of Raphael Holinshed's *Chronicles*. Holinshed and a number of contributing editors prepared a compendious encyclopaedia of England, Scotland and Ireland, with information on the history, geography and culture of Britain drawn from a large array of earlier sources. Shakespeare used the second edition of this text printed in 1587, perhaps by arrangement with his fellow Stratford emigrant, the printer Richard Field, who had published Shakespeare's first book *Venus and Adonis* (1593) and whose backlist of works by Ovid, Plutarch and Greene included many of Shakespeare's favourite source-texts. These were expensive books – Holinshed is in multiple volumes – and it is unlikely that Shakespeare owned his own library of sources.

In writing about the Scottish regicide and tyrant Macbeth under a Scottish king and patron, Shakespeare needed to find an episode of Scottish history that was not, as most of them were, entirely about wars with England. In the fifth volume of Holinshed's *Chronicles,* the story of Macbeth, spliced with material about the death of King Duff, presented Shakespeare with the materials for a play that could be appreciated both in the public theatres and at the Stuart court. It was a difficult balancing act, and critics have tended to over-emphasize the play as directed towards James, when its first, and potentially more significant audience, were the Bankside regulars at the Globe theatre.

The pro-Scottish temper of the new administration was not necessarily shared by all of James' English subjects, who were resistant to ideas about uniting the two kingdoms and suspicious of James' preferment of Scottish earls (it may be that Malcolm's 'Henceforth be Earls; the first that ever Scotland/ In such an honour nam'd' (5.9.29–30) nodded at contemporary controversy, rather than being merely part of his bland accession to power). In a speech in Parliament, Sir Christopher Piggot spoke against the Scots and used their violent history against them, asserting that they 'have not suffered above two kings to die in their beds, these two hundred years' (McLuskie, 63). He was imprisoned in the Tower of London at the King's insistence, but a popular satiric poem urged support for his views: 'if you fart at the union [between England and Scotland] remember Kitt Piggott'. The theatre was also a prominent satiric voice. For their part in anti-Scottish comic material in the play *Eastward Ho*, performed in 1605, the year before Macbeth, Ben Jonson and George Chapman were imprisoned. Even a passing joke about the 'Scottish Lord' in Elizabethan editions of Shakespeare's own *The Merchant of Venice* is carefully neutralized in the 1623 Folio text to 'other Lord' (1.2.75). The King's Men had fallen foul of sensitivities about Scottish history with a play called *The Tragedy of Gowrie*, which presumably dramatized an attempt on James' life by the Earl of Gowrie in 1600, and was suppressed by the authorities so successfully after two performances that no copy of the play has survived. Treatment of the Scots was thus a delicate business. As well as addressing himself to James' genealogy and to his interests in witchcraft and in the nature of kingship (the King had published on both these subjects before his accession to the English throne), therefore, we might see that Shakespeare winks at the home audience in his vision of a Scotland that can only be redeemed from tyranny and brutality by England.

Shakespeare's main alterations to his source material can be placed under three headings. First, characterological: Shakespeare deepens and complicates Macbeth's character and builds up Lady Macbeth out of the merest suggestions found in two different wives in Holinshed. Secondly, dramaturgical: events are condensed and compressed to create a fast-paced study of consequences, in contrast to the period of peaceful rule attributed to King Macbeth in Holinshed. Thirdly, political. Shakespeare turns Duncan from an inept Scottish warlord into a sanctified figure of divine rule, and changes Banquo from accomplice to bystander. He reshapes Holinshed's narrative of violent Scottish succession – Christopher Piggott was right: Shakespeare could find any number of regicides and rebellions in the pages preceding the history of King Macbeth – and suggests that the murder of a king is an exceptional act of moral failing, rather than a commonplace piece of realpolitik. In addition, the role of the witches is amplified in the play to stress the supernatural element of the story and to imply a broader cosmic struggle between the forces of good and evil.

All of these elements are discussed in more detail below; all of these changes are, first and foremost, linguistic ones. In reading what Shakespeare read as he prepared his play, we can see elements of vocabulary and phrasing that he kept, as well as many times when his own linguistic imagination transformed the prose of the historical source. This exercise in comparison makes us more attentive to the work particular words and phrases do in constructing plot and character.

The character of Macbeth in Holinshed is a much less complex and interior protagonist than he is in Shakespeare. Holinshed's interest is in the what and when of history: Shakespeare's is more in the why or how, and thus the play can be cavalier with historical facts in order to get to dramatic verities. Holinshed presents a Macbeth akin to the one whose exploits are described so admiringly in the play's 1.2; the reflective, solitary, even morose figure of Macbeth from 1.3 onwards is a Shakespearean invention. In his film, Roman Polanski introduces Jon Finch with an extreme closeup of his moody face, zooming back to include the backdrop of the hanged rebels swinging from their gallows: the effect is of a man quite different from the active, unthinking fighter discussed previously. But if Shakespeare interiorizes Macbeth he also leaves out some of the elements in Holinshed's account that make Macbeth a more sympathetic politician. Part of King Macbeth's job in the chronicles is to make good the 'enormities and abuses which had chanced through the feeble and slothful administration of Duncan', and Holinshed describes how he punishes those who 'most oppressed the commons'. 'The people enjoying the blissful benefit of good peace and tranquility', Macbeth 'was accounted the sure defence and buckler [shield] of innocent people'. The historical Macbeth reigned for 17 years. 'To be brief', Holinshed summarizes, 'such were the worthy doings and princely acts of this Macbeth in the administration of the realm, that if he had attained thereunto by rightful means and continued in uprightness of justice as he began, till the end of his reign, he might well have been numbered among the most noble princes that anywhere had reigned'.

This praise of Macbeth as a ruler in Holinshed is completely absent from Shakespeare's play, in which the murder of Duncan means that Macbeth has forfeited any claim to just government. If for Holinshed Macbeth's route to the crown was at odds with his occupying of it, Shakespeare reconciles this apparent discrepancy, making Macbeth's kingship over his 'poor country' a 'tyranny': (4.3.31–2): 'I think our country sinks beneath the yoke,/ It weeps, it bleeds; and each new day a gash/ Is added to her wounds' (4.3.39–41). In some ways, we could say that Shakespeare has made a more monarchical and politically conventional drama out of source material which acknowledges more contradiction in Macbeth's historical role. Sir Philip Sidney's Elizabethan defence of 'poetry' (by which he means fiction of all types, including drama), against the moral claims of history and philosophy, is relevant here: 'that which is commonly attributed to the praise of history, in respect of the notable learning is gotten by marking the success, as though therein a man should see virtue exalted and vice punished – truly that commendation is peculiar to poetry and far off from history' (Sidney, 225). History, writes Sidney, does not give us the simple moral we might seek; only fiction can do that. Shakespeare uses the liberty of fiction, we might argue, to clarify the play's moral compass.

If Shakespeare leaves out Holinshed's praise of Macbeth, he does the opposite with Duncan, constructing him as an ideal king in contrast to the source. Holinshed describes Duncan as 'of too soft a nature', and compares him with his cousin Macbeth: 'where the one had too much of clemency and the other of cruelty, the mean virtue betwixt these two extremities, might have reigned by indifferent partition in them both'. In the chronicle, Duncan is seen to be responsible for the rebellion against him, since he was 'negligent in punishing offenders' so that 'many misruled persons took occasion thereof to trouble the peace and quiet state of the commonwealth by seditious commotions'. When Duncan raises an army to defeat the rebels, Holinshed remarks: 'Sometimes it happeneth, that a dull coward and slothful person, constrained by necessity, becometh very hardy and active.' Macdonwald taunts him as a 'Faint-hearted milksop, more meet to govern a sort of idle monks in some cloister than to have the rule of such valiant and hardy men of war as the Scots were'. None of this makes it into Shakespeare's play, where no criticism of Duncan is permitted. Instead the characteristics that are identified as weakness in the source become a kind of virtue in the play: Duncan 'hath borne his faculties so meek' (1.7.17) and even his corpse is precious, with 'silver skin lac'd with his golden blood' (2.3.210). He is often played on the stage as a wise and virtuous old man, as in Rupert Goold's production, or, as under Greg Doran's direction at the RSC in 1999, dressed in striking, dazzling white and golden robes against the drab background of his thanes. Duncan shimmers in the gloom that encircles Trevor Nunn's 1979 television version. When Macbeth later appeared in the same consecrated white robes worn by an explicitly religious Duncan in Peter

Hall's production, one reviewer reported 'the blasphemy was shocking' (Wilders, 67). By contrast, Roman Polanski's film demystifies Duncan by presenting him in armour on horseback travelling through the post-battle devastation while the victors steal from the bodies of the fallen, his laughter at the account of Macbeth's violence ringing across the desolate beach. A modern version for BBC television, titled *Macbeth on the Estate* (dir. Penny Woolcock, 1997) also bucks the theatrical trend and instead raids Holinshed for a prologue stressing the violence of the play-world and refusing the ideological comforts of Shakespeare's reinvention of the saintly Duncan:

> I tell of a time not long past, when Duncan, the king, held the power on this estate and we loved him well. We was men of war – Macbeth, Banquo, Ross – we punished offenders and gathered all finances due to the king. But in time Duncan grew fat, slack, and many misruled man took occasion to trouble the peace with seditious commotion. We were assailed by rebels. Fearful of his crown, Duncan charged his cousin, the ever-loyal Macbeth, to take up arms and lead us into battle against them.

An overweight, rough-looking Duncan (played by Ray Winstone, well-known for tough, working-class roles) sits smoking restlessly in the estate social club awaiting news of the battle, pictured as a terrifying attack on a household conducted by Macbeth and Banquo armed with baseball bats. This Macbeth is closer to Holinshed's in stripping out Shakespeare's sanctification of the reigning king, and gives us a real sense of what a dramatized version of the chronicle might look like. *Macbeth on the Estate* imagines Scotland as a dog-eat-dog world constructed around male violence, in which might is more important than right; Shakespeare, by contrast, overlays the violent world of eleventh-century history with James' own political philosophy of the divine right of kings (itself a useful fiction to prop up the Stuart claim to the throne), establishing Duncan as a righteous and rightful ruler, whose death is 'most sacrilegious Murther [which] hath broke ope/ The Lord's anointed Temple' (2.3.67–8). The moral stakes of the murder are ratcheted up through the religious language.

Two extracts from Holinshed

We can see something of how Shakespeare expands, elaborates, copies and compresses his source material by looking closely at the sequence in which Banquo and Macbeth encounter the witches. Here's the section from Holinshed, with spelling and punctuation modernized:

I Banquo and Macbeth and the fairies

Shortly after happened a strange and uncouth wonder, which afterward was the cause of much trouble in the realm of Scotland, as ye shall after hear. It fortuned as Macbeth and Banquo journeyed towards Forres, where the king then lay, they went sporting by the way together without other company, save only themselves, passing thorough the woods and fields, when suddenly in the midst of a land, there met them three women in strange and wild apparel, resembling creatures of elder world, whom when they attentively beheld, wondering much at the sight, the first of them spake and said; All hail Macbeth, thane of Glamis (for he had lately entered into that dignity and office by the death of his father Sinell). The second of them said; Hail Macbeth thane of Cawdor. But the third said; All hail Macbeth that hereafter shalt be king of Scotland.

Then Banquo: What manner of women (saith he) are you; that seem so little favourable unto me, whereas to my fellow here, besides high offices, ye assign also the kingdom, appointing forth nothing for me at all & Yes (saith the first of them) we promise greater benefits unto thee, than unto him, for he shall reign in deed, but with an unlucky end: neither shall he leave any issue behind him to succeed in his place, where contrarily thou in deed shalt not reign at all, but of thee those shall be borne which shall govern the Scottish kingdom by long order of continual descent. Herewith the foresaid women vanished immediately out of their sight.

This was reputed at the first but some vain fantastical illusion by Macbeth and Banquo, insomuch that Banquo would call Macbeth in jest, king of Scotland; and Macbeth again would call him in sport likewise, the father of many kings. But afterwards the common opinion was, that these women were either the weird sisters, that is (as ye would say) the goddesses of destiny, or else some nymphs or fairies, indued with knowledge of prophesy by their necromantical science, because everything came to pass as they had spoken. For shortly after, the thane of Cawdor being condemned at Forres of treason against the king committed; his lands, livings and offices were given of the king's liberality to Macbeth.

The same night after, at supper, Banquo jested with him and said; Now Macbeth thou hast obtained those things which the two former sisters prophesied, there remaineth only for thee to purchase that which the third said should come to pass. Whereupon Macbeth revolving the thing in his mind, began even then to devise how he might attain to the kingdom: but yet he thought with himself that he must tarry a time, which should advance him thereto (by the divine providence) as it had come to pass in his former preferment. But shortly after it chanced that king Duncan, having two sons by his wife which was the daughter of Siward earl of Northumberland, he made the elder of them called Malcolm prince of Cumberland, as it were thereby to appoint him his successor in the kingdom, immediately after his decease. Macbeth sore troubled herewith, for that he saw by this means his hope sore hindered (where, by the old laws of the realm, the ordinance was, that if he that should succeed were not of able age to take the charge upon himself, he that was next of blood unto him should be admitted) he began to take counsel how he might usurp the kingdom by force, having a just quarrel so to do (as he took the matter) for that Duncan did what in him lay to defraud him of all manner of title and claim, which he might in time to come, pretend unto the crown.

The words of the three weird sisters also (of whom before ye have heard) greatly encouraged him hereunto, but specially his wife lay sore upon him to attempt the thing, as she that was very ambitious, burning in unquenchable desire to bear the name of a queen. At length therefore, communicating his purposed intent with his trusty friends, amongst whom Banquo was the chiefest, upon confidence of their promised aid, he slew the king at Enverns, or (as some say) at Botgosvane, in the sixth year of his reign.

Shakespeare's working methods are revealing here, at the micro-level of the sentence as well as the macro-level of plot and motivation. Many of the details are carried over: they are on their way to Forres, for instance (this is the only reference to this place–name in the play); Macbeth's father Sinell is named for the only time; the word 'fantastical' is picked up. We can see, for example, how Shakespeare recasts the witches' greetings into verse lines, adding the repetition of 'hail' and deploying the rhetorical trope of anaphora (the repetition of the same word or words at the beginning of successive lines) to tighten the magical or performative effect. Shakespeare follows Holinshed in having Banquo take the lead in interviewing the witches, but both his speech and their replies are more formal: 'If you can look into the seeds of time,/ And say which grain will grow, and which will not,/ Speak then to me' (1.3.58–60) is a metaphor of growth and fruition associated elsewhere in the play with Duncan and his tree-bearing heirs, and firmly distinguished from the 'barren sceptre' (3.1.61) of Macbeth's own rule. The witches reply with the three-fold repetition established by their words to Macbeth, a more dramatic reiteration than Holinshed's description of the first of them only talking to Banquo. Their words are more riddling and enigmatic in the play than in the chronicle, where they explain clearly that Macbeth will come to an 'unlucky end' and will not have any heirs.

Shakespeare picks up from Holinshed that Macbeth and Banquo joke about what has been promised – here they do it not after supper but immediately, and their 'jest' has an uneasy edge of nervousness. Polanski has the two men laughing together as they gallop away from the encounter. 'Common opinion' in Holinshed suggests that these prophecies are widely known, whereas they seem a secret held by Banquo, Macbeth and Lady Macbeth in the play. The chronicle pre-empts the fulfilment of the witches' predictions: 'everything came to pass as they had spoken'. Although the play does not speak this certainty until Banquo's 'Thou hast it now, King, Cawdor, Glamis, all,/ As the Weird Women promis'd' (3.1.1–2), perhaps events are also already inevitable here. But Shakespeare, as discussed in more detail in the next chapter, inverts the order of events in Holinshed: the treachery of the Thane of Cawdor is already revealed to the audience in 1.2, before the witches tell Macbeth he will succeed to the title. Here, as in Orson Welles' film, the prophecy comes first. This has implications for the issue of agency and control in the play (see Chapter Three), and the chronicle seems to attribute responsibility for Macbeth's actions more clearly than does Shakespeare: here the Weird Sisters' words encourage him, but so too does his ambitious wife. From this suggestion, Shakespeare develops the scene of Lady Macbeth's response to the letter, but he does not bring out her personal ambition. Her first soliloquy is all about him: the words 'thou' and 'thy' occur 13 times; 'me', 'I' and 'my' a mere 4 (1.5.14–29). Holinshed's Macbeth wonders if he will become king 'by divine providence'; Shakespeare's relies on the less sanctified notion of 'Chance' (1.3.144).

The suggestion of Macbeth 'revolving the thing in his mind' gave Shakespeare Macbeth's withdrawn demeanour in

1.4, but also, perhaps, his inability to name the deed: 'the thing'. But Holinshed's Macbeth already has a justified political claim to the throne as his cousin Duncan attempts to disinherit him by appointing Malcolm Prince of Cumberland; for Shakespeare the identification of a ruler's eldest son as his heir seems entirely natural, the law of primogeniture intrinsic to ideas of monarchical succession. By contrast with his historical precedent, the play's Macbeth does not 'take counsel': by contrast, his immediate reaction is to withdraw into the asides that structure his presence in the second half of 1.4, and the soliloquies which dominate subsequently. Shakespeare turns Macbeth into a tragic hero by isolating him, a process which begins as he turns away from conversation immediately after hearing from the witches. Holinshed's Macbeth works with 'trusty friends': the aftermath of Duncan's murder is that 'by common consent' he was crowned at Scone, unlike the play, where Macduff, at least, is resistant to it in a strained dialogue with Ross at the end of Act 2.

Perhaps the biggest difference between the two versions of the story is the treatment of Duncan's death. In Holinshed it is brusquely conveyed, unlike its dilated depiction in the play. Shakespeare patches the story here with details from an earlier king, whose murder gives the play its emotional and dramatic texture. King Duff is at Donewald's castle, 'having a special trust in Donewald, as a man whom he never suspected' (remember Duncan's 'he was a gentleman on whom I built/ An absolute trust'?) Donewald's wife encourages him 'to make him [the king] away, and shewed him the means whereby he might soonest accomplish it. Donewald thus being the more kindled in wrath by the words of his wife, determined to follow her advice in the execution of so heinous an act.' Donewald's wife gives Shakespeare more clues to the character of Lady Macbeth, and the assassination of King Duff feeds the events in Dunsinane:

In the morning when the noise was raised in the king's chamber how the king was slain, his body conveyed away

and the bed all berayed with blood, he with the watch ran
thither as though he had known nothing of the matter, and
breaking into the chamber and finding cakes of blood in
the bed & on the floor about the sides of it, he forthwith
slew the chamberlains, as guilty of that heinous murder,
and then like a mad man running to and fro, he ransacked
every corner within the castle, as though it had been to
have seen if he might have found either the body or any of
the murderers hid in any privy place: but at length coming
to the postern gate, & finding it open, he burdened the
chamberlains whom he had slain with all the fault, they
having the keys of the gates committed to their keeping
all the night and therefore it could not be otherwise (said
he) but that they were of counsel in the committing of that
most detestable murder. Finally such was his over-earnest
diligence in the inquisition and trial of the offenders herein,
that some of the Lords began to mislike the matter, and to
smell forth shrewd tokens, that he should not be altogether
clear himself [. . .]. For the space of six months together
after this heinous murder thus committed, there appeared
no sun by day, nor moon by night in any part of the realm,
but still was the sky covered with continual clouds, and
sometimes such outrageous winds arose with lightnings
and tempests, that the people were in great fear of present
destruction.

Looking at the details Shakespeare chooses to leave out from
his sources is as revealing as seeing the borrowings. What in
Holinshed is a gorily realistic description of the murdered
king's bed caked in blood is in Shakespeare a poetic invocation
of 'his silver skin lac'd with his golden blood' (2.3.110); what
unfolds as a sustained charade of blaming the chamberlains
with 'over-earnest diligence' is in the play a truncated atmosphere of suspicion and unvoiced recrimination, curtailed,
perhaps, by Lady Macbeth's strategic faint. But what we can
see is a writer poring over the history of Scotland to shape an
exciting story of regicide and its retribution, stitching together

different episodes to flesh out the role of Lady Macbeth and the aftermath of the murder, and picking out specific linguistic details as well as broader dramaturgical possibilities. The sections quoted here do not exhaust the evidence of Shakespeare's reading of Holinshed: you can read the entire text of the 1587 text of Holinshed online and see more of what Shakespeare has picked up and discarded in crafting his play (the history of Scotland is in Volume 5).

II Malcolm and Macduff

Above, we discussed the difficulties of the scene in which Malcolm and Macduff discuss kingship in England. Does it make a difference to that analysis if we compare it with the passage from Holinshed that Shakespeare is adapting?

[Malcolm:] I am truly very sorry for the misery chanced to my country of Scotland, but though I have never so great affection to relieve the same, yet by reason of certain incurable vices, which reign in me, I am nothing meet thereto. First, such immoderate lust and voluptuous sensuality (the abominable fountain of all vices) followeth me, that if I were made king of Scots, I should seek to deflower your maids and matrons, in such wise that mine intemperancy should be more importable unto you, than the bloody tyranny of Macbeth now is. Here unto Macduff answered: This surely is a very evil fault, for many noble princes and kings have lost both lives and kingdoms for the same; nevertheless there are women enow in Scotland, and therefore follow my counsel. Make thyself king, and I shall convey the matter so wisely, that thou shalt be so satisfied at thy pleasure in such secret wise, that no man shall be aware thereof.

Then said Malcolm, I am also the most avaricious creature on the earth, so that if I were king, I should seek so many ways to get lands and goods, that I would slay the most part of all the nobles of Scotland by surmised accusations, to the end I might enjoy their lands, goods, and possessions; and therefore to show you what mischief may ensue on you through mine insatiable covetousness. I will rehearse unto you a fable. There was a [fox] for having a sore place on her overset with a swarm of flies, that continually sucked out her blood: and when one that came by and saw this manner, demanded whether she would have the flies driven beside her, she answered no: for if these flies that are already full, and by reason thereof suck not very eagerly, should be chased away, other that are empty and felly and hungered, should light in their places, and suck out the residue of my blood far more to my grievance than these, which now being satisfied do not much annoy me. Therefore saith Malcolm, suffer me to remain where I am, least if I attain to the regiment of your realm, mine unquenchable avarice may prove such; that ye would think the displeasures which now grieve you, should seem easy in respect of the unmeasurable outrage, which might ensue through my coming amongst you.

Macduff to this made answer, how it was a far worse fault than the other:

. . . for avarice is the root of all mischief, and for that crime the most part of our kings have been slain and brought to their final end. Yet notwithstanding follow my counsel, and take upon thee the crown. There is gold and riches enough in Scotland to satisfy thy greedy desire. Then said Malcolm again, I am furthermore inclined to dissimulation, telling of leasings, and all other Dissimulation and kinds of deceit, so that I naturally rejoice in nothing so much, as to betray & deceive such as put any trust or confidence in my words. Then sith there is nothing that more becometh a prince than constancy, verity, truth, and justice, with the other laudable fellowship of those faire and noble virtues which are comprehended only in soothfastness, and that lying utterly overthroweth the same; you see how unable I am to govern any province or region: and therefore sith you have remedies to cloak and hide all the rest of my other vices, I pray you find shift to cloak this vice amongst the re[st].

Then said Macduff: This yet is the worst of all, and there I leave thee, and therefore say: Oh ye unhappy and miserable Scottishmen, which are thus scourged with so many and sundry calamities, each one about other! Ye have one cursed and wicked tyrant that now reigneth over you, without any right or title, oppressing you with his most bloody cruelty. This other that hath the right to the crown, is so replete with the inconstant behaviour and manifest vices of Englishmen, that he is nothing worthy to enjoy it: for by his own confession he is not only avaricious, and given to insatiable lust, but so false a traitor withal, that no trust is to be had unto any word he speaketh. Adieu Scotland, for now I account myself a banished man for ever, without comfort or consolation: and with those words brackish tears trickled down his cheeks very abundantly.

At the last, when he was ready to depart, Malcolm took him by the sleeve, and said: Be of good comfort Macduff, for I have none of these vices before remembered, but have jested with thee in this manner, only to prove thy mind: for diverse times heretofore hath Macbeth sought by this manner of means to bring me into his hands, but the more slow I have showed myself to condescend to thy motion and request, the more diligence shall I use in accomplishing the same.

Incontinently hereupon they embraced each other, and promising to be faithful the one to the other, they fell in consultation how they might best provide for all their business, to bring the same to good effect.

It's clear that Shakespeare works closely with this extract to structure the conversation in 4.3 of his play. It must have been open on his writing desk as he wrote *Macbeth*. Again, we can see how he reshapes prose dialogue into verse, using literary devices as rhetorical ornament (see Chapter One). He stresses the kingly virtues by adding another two lines with eight additional qualities not found in Holinshed, as well as reordering the ones he found to bring out the blank verse rhythm. It's interesting to see that Shakespeare discards Malcolm's rather scabrous simile of the fox bothered by flies, which in Holinshed is used to indicate that Scotland, like the fox, would be better off with a sated tyrant/fly than a new invigorated king/parasite: why do you think he chooses to omit the comparison? Shakespeare's Macduff does not cry at this news – it is the intelligence about his 'pretty chickens, and their dam' (4.3.218), that prompts the tears that in this play so concerned with correct gender roles, are indicated as feminine: 'I could play the woman with mine eyes' (4.3.230). Holinshed has no need to gloss Macduff's distress in this normative way. It's clear, too, that Shakespeare does not give us the happy resolution to this test: there is no time in the structure of the scene for the embracing, promising and planning that for Holinshed re-establishes the relationship between the two men. In the chronicle, Macbeth's attack on Macduff's family has already happened – it is Macbeth's revenge because Macduff refuses to take his turn in the building of a new stronghold 'on top of an high hill called Dunsinane', and this becomes the spur for Macduff to leave for England to try to rouse support against Macbeth. Holinshed's character is thus not tainted with the suggestion of having saved his own skin as is Shakespeare's.

Originality

Before we leave this investigation of Shakespeare's borrowings, a final word on the question of originality. The argument above suggests we have our best chance to observe Shakespeare in the act of artistic creation when we look at his work with his source-material. But if your own critical writing were to be so influenced by prior work as Shakespeare is by Holinshed, you would be guilty of plagiarism. As you already know, all sources for your own critical prose – including this book – must now be fully acknowledged, whether they have been quoted directly or summarized in paraphrase. My own institution, the University of Oxford, advises students sternly that 'Plagiarism is a breach of academic integrity. It is a principle of intellectual honesty that all members of the academic community should acknowledge their debt to the originators of the ideas, words and data which form the basis for their own work. Passing off another's work as your own is not only poor scholarship, but also means that you have failed to complete the learning process. Deliberate plagiarism is unethical and can have serious consequences for your future career; it also undermines the standards of your institution and of the degrees it issues.' Relying on other writers isn't just a failure of originality in these strictures: it's an ethical betrayal. So don't try this at home.

But for Shakespeare and his era, the underlying notions of intellectual property and of the value of originality do not pertain. The new word 'playwright' – the *OED*'s earliest citation is within months of the date of *Macbeth* – much like its precedent 'playmaker', stresses the work of the dramatist as assemblage, working with raw materials: it is formed on the verbal model of 'shipwright' – a shipbuilder – or 'wheelwright' – one who fashions wheels. The emphasis, then, is more artisanal than imaginative, more about working with raw materials to shape them into commodities than about the flash of inspiration we associate with the poetic models we have inherited from the Romantic period. Shakespeare's work with Holinshed is as much 'wrighting', construction, as it is 'writing', verbal expression.

Speed, anticipation and fulfilment

If the play's structure shares some aspects of the pacing of horror films, its overriding impulse is headlong. Words relating to time are studded throughout *Macbeth* (perhaps surprisingly, there are more of these than there are words relating to blood). So too are numbers: Banquo's 'twenty trenched gashes' (3.4.26), the line of eight kings, the ten thousand men supplied by King Edward of England. These represent two related ways to control the action and to support the play's architecture of scene and plot.

Some of the play's speed is literalized. The captain speaks out his account of the battle until he is 'faint, my gashes cry for help' (1.2.43). In Rupert Goold's television film of the play the captain is clearly mortally wounded, being rushed down an underground corridor in a makeshift field hospital with artillery shells booming above them: the desperate gasp in his tone is audible, as he uses his last breaths to deliver his message. He is wheeled off by a trio of nurses in surgical masks, who become the witches, killing him and plucking his heart from his chest to serve in their spells. The captain's speech is striking as the only extended passage of past-tense narration in a play studded with present and future. News of Macbeth's fearlessness 'as thick as hail/ Came post with post' (1.3.97–8); the messenger was 'almost dead for breath' (1.5.36) trying to beat him home, where, as Duncan reports, Macbeth 'rides well;/ And his great love, sharp as his spur, hath holp him/ To his home before us' (1.6.22–4). Within minutes of hearing the witches' greetings, Macbeth is 'rapt' (1.3.143), speaking the asides that register his immediate alienation and inwardness. The gaps in the play between thought and deed, or between action and consequence, close up just as Lady Macbeth bids: 'make thick my blood,/ Stop up th'access and passage to remorse;/ That no compunctious visitings of Nature/ Shake my fell purpose, nor keep peace between/ Th'effect and it' (1.5.42–6).

Compounding 'th'effect and it' is one of the play's characteristic and expeditious modes. Frank Kermode writes that 'the first part of the play is set in a time when there is still a gap between the thought and the deed, and its language enacts this dizzying gap' (Kermode, 203), but the impulse of the play's language is to connect thought and deed. Musing on the witches' words, Macbeth struggles to maintain his hold in the present: the 'earnest of success' (1.4.132) promised him devours the current moment and he virtually ignores Ross and Banquo: 'Present fears/ Are less than horrible imaginings' (1.3.137–8): the future is a frightening place.

But he is also impatient for that future: 'Glamis, and Thane of Cawdor:/ The greatest is behind' (1.3.115–6): the sequence is already inexorable. As Emrys Jones identifies, 'his own suspense, his unbearably keen interest in the "future", is analogous to ours – hence the unrivalled sense of complicity which Macbeth generates in an audience' (Jones, 207). We, like Macbeth, are hungry for the satisfaction of the plot being fulfilled: our narrative pleasure and his ambition seek the same end. Repeated invocations of the two assertions that are immediately true make us all, audience and hero, restive for the third: 'Glamis thou art, and Cawdor; and shalt be/What thou art promised' (1.5.14–5); 'Great Glamis! worthy Cawdor!/ Greater than both, by the all-hail hereafter!' (1.5.53–4). The third term cannot be named directly, but hangs in the air, like an imperative. Jones again: 'this pattern of an unfinished triad has an irresistible power: it agitates the nerves like an unfinished sentence, and has the effect of making not only Macbeth but ourselves long to complete it' (Jones, 207).

The archetypal role of three in storytelling, from 'Goldilocks and the Three Bears' to modern cinematic trilogies such as *The Hobbit* (dir. Peter Jackson, 2012–14) is a familiar one. So too is the usefulness of deploying three equal elements in rhetoric: Aristotle identified ethos, logos and pathos as the components of effective speaking and groups of three recur in slogans and memorable quotations: Liberté, fraternité, egalité', as the French Revolutionaries had it, or 'Friends, Romans, countrymen' (3.2.74), from Shakespeare's expert rhetorician in *Julius Caesar*, Mark Anthony (to whom Macbeth likens himself in 3.154–5). But another Aristoteliean notion, that of syllogism is also relevant here. A syllogism is a deductive philosophical argument with two premises and a proposition or conclusion that appears to follow necessarily from it. 'All men are mortal; Socrates is a man; Socrates is mortal'. Macbeth responds to the witches' three assertions along the unfolding argumentative axis of a syllogism. The witches speak truth. They say I will be king. That I will be king is the truth. He is already Thane of Glamis. He shortly becomes Thane of Cawdor. Therefore he must logically become king.

Something similarly anticipatory happens to Lady Macbeth on hearing of events from her husband's letter: 'Thy letters have transported me beyond/ This ignorant present, and I feel know/ The future in the instant' (1.5.55–7). Present, future and instant are collapsed into one: 'Duncan comes here to-night' (1.5.58). Lady Macbeth predicts the end of time: her future is no future for the king: 'never/Shall sun that morrow see' (1.5.59–60). Sian Thomas, Lady Macbeth in Dominic Cooke's 2004 production, notes 'the irony is that in an instant everything does change: in the instant it takes to kill Duncan. she is done for, and she and her husband become a couple not with a future but with a terrible past which they cannot escape' (Dobson, 101). Like his wife, Macbeth wants a deed without 'consequence' – an action of the moment which can 'be the be-all and the end-all' (1.7.3, 5). Simon Russell Beale identified Macbeth's first soliloquy in 1.7 as expressing his desire to 'jump the life to come': 'As part of the bargain, he is willing, or rather wants, to live only in the present, with no past (where there is a dead child), or the future (where there should be another child, an heir)' (Dobson, 116): the issue of children is discussed in Chapter Three. For Russell Beale and his production (directed by John Caird), the play's tenses were articulated via the Macbeth marriage and its childlessness: like many of the interpretations of the play discussed in the next chapter, the unspeakable past of his characterization was the loss of a child, and the unbearable future the absence of any successor. This factor in the play makes its speed hollow, since it is proceeding towards a no-future.

This burden of the past and the evaporation of the future put considerable strain on the play's present. The early scenes of the play depict the nervy, strung-out time between thought and the deed. Even the Porter's comic riff on drink: 'it provokes the desire, but it takes away the performance [. . .] It makes him, and it mars him; it sets him on, and it takes him off; it persuades him, and disheartens him; makes him stand to, and not stand to' (2.3.29–35) relates to this theme as it plays with ideas of a gap between desire and its execution. We see this gap in the murder of Duncan, but it becomes increasingly narrowed as the play proceeds.

Between the first suggestion that Duncan should die and the act itself five complete scenes pass (depending on when you judge Macbeth first to be contemplating murder: I am counting it from his lines at 1.3.139–40: 'my thought, whose murther yet is but fantastical/ Shakes so my single state of man', where the word 'murther', even if it does not refer here to an actual murder, brings the concept explicitly into the play's consciousness). Macbeth voices 'our fears in Banquo' at 3.1.48, when he has already arranged his interview with the murderers: an intervening scene serves to ramp up the tension, as Macbeth and Lady Macbeth discuss 'O! full of scorpions is my mind' (3.2.36), and the following scene is the attack on Banquo and Fleance. Here, then, one complete scene separates the thought and its execution. By the time we get to the plan to exterminate Macduff's line, the gap between thinking and doing has entirely collapsed: 'The castle of Macduff I will surprise. . . . This deed I'll do, before this purpose cool' (4.1.150–4). Sixty-five lines later the messenger arrives at Fife Castle urging the family to flee; immediately following him are the murderers. The family is wiped out within minutes of Macbeth's decision. Lady Macbeth's taunt that he was 'afeard/ To be the same in thine own act and valour,/ As thou art in desire' (1.7.39–41) is decisively scotched. The play accelerates, galloping towards its conclusion as Macbeth's deeds come helter-skelter; 'be it thought and done' (4.1.149): no time for regrets or for looking back: that the play leaves to Lady Macbeth.

Sleepwalking

Lady Macbeth's sleepwalking scene is the play's other major instance of retrospection (echoing the tense of the Captain's report of the battle in 1.2). It figures the past through verbal shards of memory, but the tense is insistently present: 'no more o' that, my Lord, no more o'that: you mar all with this starting' (5.1.45–6). These memories are a trap, and Lady Macbeth is compelled to relive them in her somnambulist agonies. It is also one of *Macbeth*'s few examples of prose. Only 6.5 per cent of the play's lines are in prose, which is an unusually low proportion for plays of this period (for example *Coriolanus* has 23 per cent prose and *King Lear* 27 per cent) (Crystal, 210). The other instances of prose are the reading of Macbeth's letter in 1.5 and the Porter's Scene in 2.3). Here in 5.1, it is almost as if the verse-line, already strained by the events of the play, cannot cope with her fractured memories. It reviews both events we recall from the scenes around Duncan's death, and others not shown to us, which together draw a desperate portrait of Lady Macbeth's attempts to support her husband through the crime and its aftermath, while coping herself with the trauma. It is a long way from the pragmatic 'A little water clears us of this deed' (2.2.66): instead, famously, 'out, damned spot' (5.1.36) accompanies her obsessive hand-washing. She offers her own version of Macbeth's hyperbole: 'will all great Neptune's ocean wash this blood / Clean from my hand' (2.2.59–60). Macbeth's imagination of the scale of his enormity is visual, technicolour; Lady Macbeth's is olfactory: 'Here's the smell of the blood still: all the perfumes of Arabia will not sweeten this little hand' (5.1.51–3). The sleep-walking scene displays for us Lady Macbeth's own imperfectly suppressed memories, but also serves to recover the play's own structural unconscious, reliving the moment of Duncan's death as a kind of primal scene, just as the English forces are massing to reinstate the rightful heir of the murdered king. It recalls Duncan, Banquo and Lady Macduff as 'the Thane of Fife had a wife: where is she now?' (5.1.43–4). It thus functions structurally as a kind of fulcrum between past and future. What has been sacrificed, as Lady Macbeth's agonies make clear, is any kind of secure present.

Describing Ron Daniels' production in 1999 in New York, Bernice Kliman observed that in this regard the two central protagonists swapped positions: 'she, the one who looked forward, who urged Macbeth to look to the future to success and triumph, cannot stop looking back at what they have done (especially the murder of the Macduff family), and he, who before and immediately after the murder of Duncan, looked back longingly at a life of wholeness and camaraderie, can do nothing but move forward without learning anything from the past' (Kliman, 157). The future is empty, 'And that which should accompany old age,/ As honour, love, obedience, troops of friends,/ I must not look to have' (5.3.24–6).

All Shakespeare's tragedies have a kind of apocalypse as the consequence of the action. To be alive at the end of a tragedy is a mixed blessing: it is to have survived the play's turmoil, but to have therefore been too uninteresting, too puny, to be involved in it. Thus, the literal corpse on stage in the final moments is metaphorically the corpse of the future, which is either now too compromised or too inadequate to be viable. In *Macbeth* the recognition is explicit from the play's beginning. By rushing headlong into the future and making the witches' 'shalt be' into 'is now', Macbeth's murder of Duncan becomes a murder of proper linear time. He tells Lady Macbeth that 'Strange things I have in head that will to hand,/ Which must be acted ere they may be scanned' (3.4.138–9): the tenses enact a forward movement from present ('have') through future ('will') and imperative ('must'), and the end-rhymes emphasize the same pitching onwards. What Macbeth here wants is to act before scanning ('to scan' has a number of meanings, including to discern metre in poetry, to judge or to consider deeply). He turns away from the natural seasonal imagery of time passing – Banquo's 'If you can look into the seeds of time,/ And say which grain will grow, and which will not' (1.3.58–9) – and instead into a vortex 'which o'erleaps itself/ And falls on th'other' (1.7.27–8).

No wonder, then, that the culmination of Macbeth's recognition of the futility of his position is figured in terms of disrupted or meaningless progression:

> To-morrow, and to-morrow, and to-morrow,
> Creeps in this petty pace from day to day,
> To the last syllable of recorded time;
> And all our yesterdays have lighted fools
> The way to dusty death. (5.5.19–23)

There will be no future. Time is only a word, a syllable. And to confirm the emptiness of the lines, they echo something we've already had. When Macbeth returns to the troubled thanes having viewed Duncan's murdered body, he suggests that things are already over, in a speech that seems simultaneously hypocritical (he has, of course, murdered Duncan himself) and deeply sincere (there is no going back from this):

> Had I but died an hour before this chance,
> I had lived a blessed time; for, from this instant,
> There's nothing serious in mortality;
> All is but toys: renown, and grace, is dead;
> The wine of life is drawn, and the mere lees
> Is left this vault to brag of. (2.3.89–94)

Even despair, then, is mere repetition. As Marjorie Garber puts it, 'the tension between cycle and line maps the structure of the play at every point from first to last' (Garber, 702).

Writing matters

I Holinshed as source

In analysing Shakespeare's changes to his source in Holinshed we have stressed both the things that he picks up and those which he drops. Try the exercise now comparing with the play's Act 3 this section from Holinshed which Shakespeare uses closely. Remember that you are looking at vocabulary and expression, as well as at plot and structure. How does Shakespeare extend this sequence and divide it into scenes? How does his language echo or transform Holinshed?

Shortly after, [Macbeth] began to show what he was, instead of equity practising cruelty. For the prick of conscience (as it chanceth ever in tyrants, and such as attain to any estate by unrighteous means) caused him ever to fear, least he should be served of the same cup, as he had ministered to his predecessor. The words also of the three weird sisters, would not out of his mind, which as they promised him the kingdom, so likewise did they promise it at the same time unto the posterity of Banquo. He willed therefore the same Banquo with his son named Fleance, to come to a supper that he had prepared for them, which was indeed, as he had devised, present death at the hands of certain murderers, whom he hired to execute that deed, appointing them to meet with the same Banquo and his son without the palace, as they returned to their lodgings, and there to slay them, so that he would not have his house slandered, but that in time to come he might clear himself, if any thing were laid to his charge upon any suspicion that might arise.

It chanced yet by the benefit of the dark night, that though the father were slain, the son yet by the help of almighty God reserving him to better fortune, escaped that danger: and afterwards having some inkling (by the admonition of some friends which he had in the court) how

his life was sought no less than his father's, who was slain
not by chance-medley (as by the handling of the matter
Macbeth would have had it to appear) but even upon a
prepensed [premeditated] device: whereupon to avoid
further peril he fled into Wales. [Holinshed then traces
Fleance's descendants before returning to the Macbeth
story]. After the contrived slaughter of Banquo, nothing
prospered with the foresaid Macbeth: for in manner every
man began to doubt his own life, and durst uneath [hardly]
appear in the king's presence; and even as there were many
that stood in fear of him, so likewise stood he in fear of
many, in such sort that he began to make those away by
one surmised cavillation [trick] or other, whom he thought
most able to work him any displeasure.

At length he found such sweetness by putting his nobles
thus to death, that his earnest thirst after blood in this
behalf might in no wise be satisfied.

II Time and tenses

Take two scenes from different parts of the play – maybe 1.1
and 3.6, for instance – and try to analyse their tenses (past,
present or future). Are they reporting (their conversations
refers to the past and/or uses the past tense) or anticipating
(future tenses) or enacting (present tenses)? How might we
think about this as a kind of signpost to the play's plotting –
pointing backwards or forwards, or demanding our attention
on the here and now? Are there any other words or phrases
that refer to time or speed – the time of day, or adverbs around
motion ('swiftly', 'slowly'), and if so, how might these contribute to the structure of tenses you have already identified?

III Plotting and structure

Take two, or preferably three (remember the rule of three above) film versions of the play: Welles (1948) and Polanski (1971) are recommended and easily available, but you could also look at television films by Nunn (1979) or Gold (1983) or Goold (2010), or adaptations such as *Throne of Blood* (1957), *Men of Respect* (1990) or *Shakespeare Re-Told* (2005). Online video streaming sites may have versions you can watch. Make a comparison of the last ten minutes of each of the versions. The point is to think about the conclusion of their interpretation of *Macbeth*. Questions you might ask include: how much of Shakespeare's dialogue, or its equivalent, is included? How is Malcolm characterized? Where are your sympathies in the fight between Macbeth and Macduff, and how does the film manipulate these? Is there any role for the witches? What's the last image of Macbeth that we have? What's the very final image of the film?

CHAPTER THREE

Language and character

The first chapter worked with language at the level of the word, language in the service of lines and speeches. The second chapter sketched out language as a building block for the play's dramaturgy: language in the service of plot. Here we will discuss the ways in which language creates character, and, conversely, how it works independently of individual fictional personages in the play. But let us start with perhaps the most famous aspect of *Macbeth* (how did it take us so long to get to it?): the famous curse.

The curse of *Macbeth*

For many years actors and theatre professionals have been superstitious about *Macbeth*. Google the play and you will find any number of accounts of back-stage accidents, actor injuries and other supposed effects of the curse of what is known within theatres only as 'the Scottish play'. According to the legend, any mention of the title within a theatre must be cleansed with a Shakespearean antidote, such as 'Angels and ministers of grace defend us' (*Hamlet*, 1.4.39). Elaborate historical theories about the origins of this myth, involving, variously, real daggers causing death to the actors, or real witches cursing the play for their representation, or Shakespeare himself playing the role of Lady Macbeth when the boy-actor fell ill, are endlessly circulated by journalists and actors. Jonathan Slinger, interviewed by a newspaper about his forthcoming role as Macbeth in 2011, stated that he 'had no truck' with such legends; the same paper reported four months later, rather gleefully, that he had to withdraw from the role after an accident: 'Despite previously laughing off the superstition surrounding Shakespeare's "Scottish play", Jonathan Slinger has now apparently been a victim of it. The actor has had to relinquish the title role in *Macbeth* after he was knocked off his bicycle in a collision with a car in Stratford-upon-Avon.' Inevitably the headline was 'RSC actor is hit by the curse of Macbeth.' The Simpsons 'The Regina Monologues' episode has Ian McKellen welcoming the family to the London theatre where he is performing in the play. When Homer utters the fatal word, McKellen is struck by lightning and then crushed by the falling billboard advertising his role.

In fact, as scholars have investigated, there is no basis in fact for the myth, and its founding instance, an apparent quotation from the seventeenth-century diarist and theatre-goer Samuel Pepys, turns out to have been a fraud, a joke presented by the humourist Max Beerbohm early in the twentieth century. During the past 100 years, the curse of *Macbeth* has gathered independent momentum and thus became a self-fulfilling prophecy (Maguire and Smith).

Performative language

The fact that there is no evidence to support the thespian superstitions around *Macbeth* does not mean that the famous curse is irrelevant for our reading of the play. Features of the myth such as the need for euphemism, fears of bad luck and the idea of self-fulfilling prophecies are prominent in *Macbeth* itself. Just as the myth avoids naming the play directly, so too Macbeth is unwilling to speak of the murder of Duncan, preferring a series of euphemisms like 'deed', 'taking-off' (1.7.14, 20) – akin to the circumlocutions of 'the Scottish play' and 'the Thane' or 'the Scottish king'. Characters within the play also treat Macbeth's name as if the very word has a kind of talismanic power: 'there to meet with Macbeth' (1.1.7); 'this tyrant, whose sole name blisters our tongues' (4.3.12). We might see 'the Weird Sisters' – the play's preferred term and an adjective not found elsewhere in Shakespeare's works – as another euphemism for the more powerfully negative word 'witches'.

Perhaps this relates to a more thoroughgoing anxiety about the power of words in this play. The linguistic philosopher J. L. Austin influentially developed a theory of what he called 'performatives' or 'performative utterances' in a book called *How to do things with words* (1962). For Austin, performatives are linguistic utterances that do not describe or refer outside themselves; rather, they do something directly. Speaking itself performs a kind of action: it is, as Austin puts it, a 'speech-act'. Speech-acts include such particular language-use as oaths, promises and declarations: the marriage service, or swearing an affidavit or meting out punishment to a defendant (revealingly called a 'sentence'). Speech-acts are a particular prerogative of rulers: 'No more that Thane of Cawdor shall deceive/ Our bosom interest. – Go pronounce his present death,/ And with his former title greet Macbeth' (1.2.65–7). Duncan's commands are verbal: 'pronounce', 'greet'. They are performative. The king's word is his command.

Speech-acts are also, however, associated with magic. A spell – a sequence of words which conjures up or enacts the speaker's wishes – is clearly performative in Austin's sense. There were contemporary stories that at performances of *Dr Faustus*, Christopher Marlowe's famous Elizabethan play about a magician making a pact with the devil, additional devils were counted onstage, as if the play had really conjured them up by articulating the enchantment. Perhaps it is not possible to mimic or quote spells, just as soap opera weddings never speak out the whole marriage ceremony: to utter the words is to perform them. At some early modern witch trials the supposedly magical words of which the defendants were accused were not reiterated aloud in court for fear that they would again conjure up the devil: modern depictions of magic from *The Sorcerer's Apprentice* to Harry Potter often indicate that spells are performative by having them unwittingly activated as unqualified people read aloud from dusty books. So, are the witches' words in *Macbeth* spells?

The witches' powers

For the most part the witches speak a particular rhythmical language which is distinguished from the rest of the play. The first lines of the play establish this eerie soundscape:

> When shall we three meet again?
> In thunder, lightning, or in rain?
> When the hurlyburly's done,
> When the battle's lost and won. (1.1.1–4)

The lines are short, with seven or eight syllables rather than the ten (a pentameter) usual of Shakespeare's blank verse (see Chapter One) – and their shortness is further emphasized by heavy end-rhyme which draws attention to the final words. It already sounds incantatory. As Diane Purkiss points out, these rhythms had become conventional in depicting witches in Jacobean drama, and she suggests that audiences were as attuned to these aural indicators as more modern viewers might be to visual iconography: 'like the villain's black hat in a western, the octosyllabic couplet became a simplistic convention which divides evil from good' (Purkiss, 210). This characteristic rhythm is as much a feature of the witches' appearances as the trademark clap of thunder that marks their entrances: we probably now tend to visualize the witches, in part because our culture is more ocular-centric, but the play, written for a society more used to listening, presents them within a distinctive acoustic.

Most ominous about the witches' opening scene is their plan 'to meet with Macbeth' (1.1.7). Does this suggest they control him? Or merely know where he will be and can intercept him? Directing the play in 1934, Tyrone Guthrie cut 1.1 entirely, precisely because he felt it gave the witches undue influence: 'by making the three Weird Sisters open the play, one cannot avoid the implication that they are a governing influence of the tragedy . . . Surely the grandeur of the tragedy lies in the fact that Macbeth and Lady Macbeth are ruined by precisely those qualities that make them great' (Braunmuller, 32). For Guthrie, a stress on the power of the witches takes away from the human scale of the Macbeths; for them to be puppets governed by external forces reduces their magnificence even as it allows them to shrug off some of the moral responsibility for their acts. Behind Guthrie's interpretation may be a feeling that tragedy should capture human actions and human agency, rather than supernatural direction.

When the First Witch describes how she will punish the sailor's wife, her words seem to enact the retribution: 'I'll drain him dry as hay:/ Sleep shall neither night nor day /Hang upon his penthouse lid;/ He shall live a man forbid./ Weary sev'n-nights nine times nine,/ Shall he dwindle, peak, and pine' (1.3.19–24). And when we meet the witches in Act 4 their ritualistic chanting around the cauldron suggests a spell in the process of formation: 'Round about the cauldron go;/ In the poisoned entrails throw – / Toad, that under cold stone/ Days and nights has thirty-one./ Swelter'd venom, sleeping got,/ Boil thou first i'the'charmed pot' (4.1.4–9). Syntactic inversions again emphasize the regular rhythm and rhyme scheme, and distance this form of speech from anything approaching naturalistic dialogue. In his film of the play, Orson Welles resituates 'Double, double, toil and trouble' (4.1.10) from Act 4 to the opening sequence and has the witches incant their fiendish list of ingredients over the image of the swirling cauldron from which they shape a slimy idol of Macbeth himself: it is clear from this interpretation that the witches' language is powerful, material or, in Austin's terms, performative. It's an interpretation that stresses the witches' demonic agency: Welles' Macbeth is a man formed by the witches as their creature.

If the witches' spells do have a performative power, what about their prophesies? Above, I suggested that the theatrical curse of *Macbeth* has no historical basis, and that rather its apparent corroboration in stories of near-accidents, unexpected illness and even Charlton Heston's tights catching fire having been mysteriously soaked in kerosene is a 'self-fulfilling prophecy': defined by sociologist Robert Merton as 'a false definition of the situation evoking a new behaviour which makes the original false conception come "true". This specious validity of the self-fulfilling prophecy perpetuates a reign of error. For the prophet will cite the actual course of events as proof that he was right from the very beginning' (Merton, 477). Merton's phrase 'a reign of error' is highly suggestive for *Macbeth*. So too is Karl Popper's adjacent formulation, via classical Greek tragedy, of a similar notion: 'The idea that a prediction may have influence upon the predicted event is a very old one. Oedipus, in the legend, killed his father whom he had never seen before; and this was the direct result of the prophecy which had caused his father to abandon him. This is why I suggest the name "Oedipus effect" for the influence of the prediction upon the predicted event (or, more generally, for the influence of an item of information upon the situation to which the information refers), whether this influence tends to bring about the predicted event, or whether it tends to prevent it' (Popper, 13). (In the legend of Oedipus, Oedipus's father Laius, King of Thebes, was told by the oracle that he would be killed by his own son, and so, when a son was born, he sent it away to die. Instead the son was adopted and brought up in ignorance of his birth parents. In an attempt to avoid another prophecy – that he would murder his own father and marry his mother – Oedipus travelled to Thebes where he quarrelled with Laius, not knowing who he was, and killed him. He then married Laius's widow Jocasta, again, in ignorance of his relation to her. The story does not end well.)

The role of the self-fulfilling prophecy or Oedipus effect in *Macbeth* is a complex one. The witches greet Macbeth in 1.3 with a sequence of statements:

> All hail, Macbeth! hail to thee, Thane of Glamis!
> All hail, Macbeth! hail to thee, Thane of Cawdor!
> All hail, Macbeth! that shalt be King hereafter. (1.3.48–50)

The repetitive syntactic structure of these utterances hides the fact that their relation to the known situation is different in each case. Macbeth acknowledges the truth of the first through inheritance: 'By Sinel's death I know I am Thane of Glamis' (1.3.71), but finds the second and third items of 'strange intelligence' perplexing. The audience is in a significantly different position. The business of the preceding scene, Act 1 scene 2, has been to establish the political causes of Cawdor's demise: he has been a 'most disloyal traitor' in the wars with Norway, and hence stripped of his title and sentenced to death. What seems to Macbeth a prediction in 1.3 is therefore to us merely a corroboration of something we already know: it may be mysterious *how* the witches know this, but there is nothing mysterious or supernatural about *why* it is the case. It is the result of human, not supernatural, forces.

Why is this structure of the opening scenes important? It shows us a Macbeth who apparently hears something – that he will be Thane of Cawdor – and then almost immediately experiences that it comes true: Ross announces that Duncan 'bade me, from him, call thee Thane of Cawdor' (1.3.105; another performative). What to us is the gap between command (the king's words in 1.2) and execution (the delivery of the message about Cawdor – but also, literally, Cawdor's execution) appears to Macbeth as the collapsed gap between prediction and fulfilment. This sequence retrospectively turns the greeting 'All hail, Macbeth, hail to thee Thane of Cawdor' into a prophecy, and further, suggests that the next statement, 'All hail, Macbeth, that shalt be King hereafter' is another prophecy and one that will, similarly, be fulfilled. In fact the tense of the witches' second greeting is not phrased as a future prediction but as a present fact – perhaps the witches simply know what has happened, rather than being able to predict the future. But that precise distinction is overwhelmed by the speed with which Macbeth is awarded the title of Cawdor.

So, is this a kind of Oedipus effect or self-fulfilling prophecy? The role of the witches in knowing, or shaping, what will happen in the play is an ambiguous one, as discussed in the previous chapter. One the one hand, *Macbeth* is the Shakespearean tragedy in which there is least ethical doubt about the behaviour of the protagonist: everyone, including Macbeth, knows that killing Duncan is a crime. As Michael Goldman puts it, 'The experience of the play puts us inside Macbeth's head as he finds himself wholly committed to deeds whose moral abhorrence he registers with the intensest sensitivity' (Goldman, 110). On the other, it is the play in which Shakespeare most closely and perplexingly investigates the question of agency – of who or what makes the things that happen, happen. Do the witches merely anticipate, or do they effect, what happens in the future, or to put it another way, can there be any prophecy that is not 'self-fulfilling'?

Macbeth considers this amid the thrill of his responses to the news that 'I am Thane of Cawdor': 'If Chance will have me King, why Chance may crown me,/ Without my stir' (1.3.132, 144–5). Perhaps he need do nothing to allow the prophecy to be fulfilled. But the prophecy may, of course, have already anticipated the other factors at play: Macbeth's own ambition; Lady Macbeth's encouragement; the flight of Malcolm and Donalbain. That one might hear a prophecy and not act upon it may be the reason Banquo is presented as he is. In Holinshed, Shakespeare's source, the military companions Macbeth and Banquo are accomplices in the murder of the king; here, Banquo is exempted from blame. He has heard that his children shall be kings, and appears to undertake no action to bring that about. His behaviour is not apparently changed by the prophecy in order to make it self-fulfilling: he is no Oedipus. He is not entirely immune to the encounter with the witches, however: when he tries to discuss them with Macbeth he admits he has dreamed of them (2.1.20), and his soliloquy at the beginning of Act 3 hints that their words gnaw at him:

> it was said,
> It should not stand in thy posterity;
> But that myself should be the root and father
> Of many kings. If there come truth from them,
> (As upon thee, Macbeth, their speeches shine),
> Why, by the verities on thee made good
> May they not be my oracles as well,
> And set me up in hope? (3.1.3–10)

But the point is that Banquo hears a prophecy and does not obviously change his behaviour to meet it, and thus shows that this is a possible alternative to Macbeth's chosen course of action.

The question of agency

Theories of causation or agency in the early modern period in which Shakespeare wrote are complex. As an example we might look at a contemporary document, Robert Burton's encyclopaedic work on melancholy with the expansive title: *The Anatomy of Melancholy, What it is: With all the Kinds, Causes, Symptoms, Prognostics and Several Cures of it. In Three Main Partitions with their several sections, members and sub-sections. Philosophically, Medicinally, Historically, Opened and Cut up* (1621). What is useful here is Burton's copious analysis of what causes melancholy, because it offers as equivalents kinds of causes modern thinking might judge incompatible. Broadly, Burton's extensive elaboration establishes three categories of causation. Melancholy may arise from within the individual himself: he may have a congenital or hereditary predisposition, or a lifestyle, such as studying too much or eating too much garlic or having too much heat in the balance of his humours, that makes him a sufferer. It may be caused by the actions of other people: those who mock him, or put him in prison, or die and make him grief-stricken or reject his love-suit. Or it may have a more cosmic or meta-physical cause, from God, the stars or the devil. We can map these three categories quite closely onto the question of causes in *Macbeth*. Is Macbeth motivated from within, by his own 'vaulting ambition' (1.7.27)? Is he persuaded to it by other people – by Lady Macbeth's taunts? Is he puppeted from out-side by those 'instruments of Darkness' (1.3.124) he comes to recognize as 'juggling fiends' (5.8.19)? In fact the play seems to present rather than to answer these questions, in a com-plex, ambiguous exploration of the internal and external driv-ers of our actions.

Bernice Kliman's account of four broad categories for *Macbeth* in performance echoes the ways the questions have been framed on stage, and offers a useful paradigm for organ-izing productions. Her first category covers interpretations in which Macbeth and Lady Macbeth's psychologies are pre-dominant: the witches are merely a catalyst or symbol of their interior conflict. Big-scale performances by actors such as Laurence Olivier and Sarah Siddons come into this category, and the BBC television film of 1982 with Nicol Williamson and Jane Lapotaire is a reviewable example. The second pro-poses 'a controlling supernatural sphere' in which events are controlled by some cosmic force such as Fate or Evil. Orson Welles' interpolation of a Holy Father (so-called in the early production scripts; he later became 'Friar') bearing a cross in his film of 1948 reframes the story within such a conflict, as do the shattered stained glass and ruined clerestory that sig-nal the English Reformation as a context for Michael Boyd's 2010 production. Thirdly, there are productions emphasiz-ing the social world of the play, in which minor characters become more prominent: the unadorned and intense film version starring Ian McKellan and Judi Dench (dir. Trevor Nunn, 1979) might exemplify this performance trend. Finally,

Kliman identifies productions which suggest the social structure informs and shapes events, as when, for example, the witches' speeches are spoken in a choric whisper by the rest of the cast in Cheek by Jowl's interpretation, presenting their prophecies as the insistent whisper of social pressure, or when Polanski establishes the brutality of Duncan's regime at the opening of his 1971 film, or when, in *Macbeth on the Estate*, the hopeless promise to a poor community of the National Lottery stands in for the witches' prediction of future glory (Kliman, xii–xiv).

The fraught question of agency gets its most explicit disciplinary framing in the modern genre of mock-trials of Macbeth. There are any number of these amateur trials reported on the internet, often as rhetorical or judicial exercises for law students. One example can stand for the type as a whole. On 17 May 2010, the *London Evening Standard* newspaper carried the headline 'Macbeth gets away with murder in all-star trial': 'In a final twist that would make Shakespeare turn in his grave Macbeth and his wife have been found not guilty of murdering King Duncan and Banquo. That was the verdict of a one-night-only mock trial at the Royal Courts of Justice in which the case against the couple was examined with actors playing the defendants, judge and key witnesses.' A cynic might say that this outcome tells us more about the ethical slipperiness of the legal profession than about Shakespeare's play, but the focus of this kind of juridical energy on *Macbeth* in particular attests to something specific about this play: its exploration of blame, guilt and causation.

Agency and blame: Character

These debates about blame and agency tend to focus critical attention on issues of character. Our tendency as modern readers is to approach Shakespeare via psychology, and certainly, as we have seen, his plays give us rich material for such an approach. Why else, for example, would Lady Macbeth reveal that she could not herself murder Duncan because he resembled her father? Like evidence that Lady Macbeth and Macbeth have apparently discussed matters outside our hearing, this revelation is a moment in the play that implies an entire world only hinted at on stage. One corollary of this preference is that we tend to associate the plays' language with individual speakers: it is a particular character who employs a specific simile or speaks in a certain way, and that unique speech pattern – what linguists call an idiolect – is crucial to our understanding of the speakers of the play as distinct psychological beings. It's a method mined to great effect by actors, eager for clues about the backstory and the motivation for their character's action, as Harriet Walter explains in the opening of her account of playing Lady Macbeth, 'Shakespeare packs the beginning of the play chock-full of character clues hidden in the language' (Walter, 9).

Actors' insights I: Early modern

Let's take this suggestion from a leading actor a bit further. Many works of Shakespearean criticism approach the language of the plays on the page much as they would encounter a poem or novel: that's to say they employ the kind of formalist approach that dominated literary scholarship for much of the twentieth century. Often, in being asked to discuss issues about the play, it seems that we are being asked to forget the variables the play delivers in performance. But even as plays are indeed texts demanding such analytic tools of interpretation and exegesis, they are also texts for actors to embody and personate. They were written by an actor – we know that Shakespeare performed roles in his own plays and those of other writers including Ben Jonson – for a theatre company whose individual and corporate strengths and weakness he knew intimately. Many modern actors suggest that Shakespeare's theatrical longevity is because he wrote with a deep understanding of the performers' perspective – unlike other playwrights with different professional backgrounds. Throughout this book we have encountered explanations from contemporary actors of their particular understanding of certain moments and motivations. This section develops this approach more sustainedly, thinking first about early modern actors and then consulting some of the exercises designed for modern classically trained actors approaching Shakespeare's language.

The first Macbeth was almost certainly Richard Burbage, in his late thirties when the play was first performed. Burbage was the King's Men's star performer, and took major Shakespearean roles including those of Hamlet, Lear and Othello. Nothing is known of the boy actor, probably aged in his early teens, who took on the role of Lady Macbeth, but given the prominent roles for strong women in the plays of this period – such as Coriolanus' warlike mother Volumnia, or the eponymous heroine of *Antony and Cleopatra* – clearly a talented youth was available for whom Shakespeare could confidently write such demanding parts. These tragic roles have an emotional range quite different from the gamine heroines such as Viola or Rosalind in his earlier comedies. The play with over 35 speaking parts was probably performed by a cast of around 13, because of the common practice of doubling. Making a casting chart – a graph with the scene numbers across the top axis and the characters' names down the lefthand one – makes clear how the play is written to manage its acting resources effectively. Characters are available for doubling so long as they are not ever on stage together or in adjacent scenes, since continuous performance meant that no actor could leave the stage and return immediately in the next scene, either as the same or a different character. Of course, if the doubled characters require substantial re-costuming, the gap between exit and re-entrance may need to be longer. Shakespeare is also adept at writing scenes to enable costume changes, such as the Porter's scene here, part of the purpose of which is to cover the time it would take Macbeth to tidy up his bloodstained clothes after the murder and make ready for his performance of innocence when the crime is discovered.

Doubling structures the play's deployment of its characters. Banquo's death precedes the need for new characters such as Menteth in the final section of the play, and thus the same actor could have played both; there is no entry for Donalbain, Malcolm's younger brother, in the play's final scenes where we might expect logically to see him: perhaps this is because the actor has been redeployed as Seyward or one of Malcolm's captains. We never see the Old Man except in 2.4; the character may be consigned to a single scene but the actor would not be, and would return for other roles as required. The same must be the case for other patchy roles such as Lennox, Duncan, the two doctors, Fleance and the Porter. And who would you cast as Seyton, the ominously named attendant of Macbeth in the final scenes, who we have never encountered before but whose name, probably pronounced 'Satan', is repeated four times in a short scene? Is it Duncan, or Banquo, or the Porter from hell gate who accompanies Macbeth's decision to 'die with harness on our back'? Nicholas Brooke points out that since there is no exit for the character when the 'cry of women' is heard offstage – he knows Lady Macbeth has died without apparently leaving the stage – perhaps the role was suggestively doubled with that of Lady Macbeth (Brooke, 86). More conventionally, there is a long stage tradition of Seyton taking up the anonymous roles of servant and messenger earlier in the play, and thus becoming a ubiquitous and trusted household retainer.

Rupert Goold's film doubled one of the witches with Lady Macbeth's gentlewoman, and the bloody captain with one of the murderers and Old Siward with another, and Duncan and the doctor. Goold's casting decisions make clear that doubling can be an interpretative lens as well as a practical necessity: Duncan, as the doctor, watches helpless over Lady Macbeth's mental agonies, as does one of the witches. It is Duncan that Macbeth asks, ironically, to heal the diseased nation ('cast/ The water of my land, find her disease,/ And purge it to a sound and pristine health' (5.3.50–2)). Fleance and young Macduff could easily be played by the same actor, perhaps also with Young Siward. If, as was probably the case in the first performances, the witches' roles were thought of as female ones, the play puts particular stress on the actors who played female roles (this seems to have been a distinct cadre within the company, rather than a more general skill): perhaps Lady Macbeth and Lady Macduff could be played by the same boy actor, or Lady Macduff and the gentlewoman who attends Lady Macbeth's sleepwalking: either would give particular poignancy to Lady Macbeth's 'the thane of Fife had a wife: where is she now?' (5.1.43–4).

Early modern actors did not have access to the full script of the plays in which they performed: probably only a single complete text was held by the book-keeper in the theatre. Because paper was expensive, because writing out copies longhand was laborious and because the existence of more copies of a play than were necessary offered the potential for unauthorized publication or rival performance, actors had only a copy of their own role. From the few surviving examples, we know that this part consisted a scroll containing the actor's lines and the last word or two of the speech preceding his as a cue. The actors did not have direct access to the rest of the play, or to anything that any other character said about theirs, other than the hints about context and role given by the cue-words. Nor would they have any indication how long to wait for their next cue – some scenes are a swift back-and-forth between two actors only, others employ more characters or longer speeches, extending the period between speeches. All these gaps and uncertainties add to the tension of the plays in performance, as actors listen carefully to one another to try to fill out their picture of the whole and of their own character. Simon Palfrey and Tiffany Stern have written about the actor's part as 'a basic building-block' of Shakespeare's craft: what follows here is indebted to their analysis in *Shakespeare in Parts*.

If we take the Macbeth actor in his opening scene and work
out what his cue-script would have looked like, we get something like this (the long lines indicate the cue lines):

———————————————————————— wound up
So foul and fair a day I have not seen.
———————————————————————— are so
Speak if you can: what are you?
———————————————————————— all hail.
Stay, you imperfect speakers, tell me more:
By Sinel's death I know I am Thane of Glamis;
But how of Cawdor? the Thane of Cawdor lives,
A prosperous gentleman; and to be King
Stands not within the prospect of belief,
No more than to be Cawdor. Say from whence
You owe this strange intelligence? or why
Upon this blasted heath you stop our way
With such prophetic greeting? – Speak, I charge you.
———————————————————————— they vanished
Into the air; and what seem'd corporal
Melted as breath into the wind. Would they had stay'd.
———————————————————————— reason prisoner
Your children shall be kings.
———————————————————————— be king
And Thane of Cawdor too; went it not so?
———————————————— Speak true?
The Thane of Cawdor lives: why do you dress me,
In borrow'd robes?
———————————————————————— overthrown him
Glamis, and Thane of Cawdor:
The greatest is behind. – Thanks for your pains. -
Do you not hope your children shall be kings,
When those that gave the Thane of Cawdor to me,
Promised no less to them?
———————————————————————— pray you.

The Macbeth actor thus has only his own lines and the cue words to understand his role as he enters the playworld. He does not know, for instance, as we do that his opening line, 'So fair and foul a day I have not seen', echoes the witches' 'fair is foul and foul is fair'. Nor does the cue-script include any of the other information the audience already knows about Macbeth: the witches' plan to meet with him, the news of his great bravery in battle.

The cues in this scene, write Palfrey and Stern, cumulatively 'paint a picture of uncanny influence, demonic temptation, and epistemological dizziness. They harp on a single string: the supernatural or supra-rational force that will draw Macbeth into action. This character thus arrives in a world where reason, custom, and empiricism have all been superseded by some barely understood, self-estranging metaphysical determinism' (Palfrey and Stern, 465). The actor also has no idea from the cue-script whether his next cue follows immediately on, or if he has a long wait for the next speech. Here, the repeated cue 'all hail' (heard in the witches' dialogue four times before the instance that forms Macbeth's cue) gives the role an edge of impatience: perhaps the actor is trying to break into Banquo's conversation, just as his letter reports to Lady Macbeth: 'I burn'd in desire to question them further' (1.5.3–4). The cues here indicate the world into which Macbeth is inducted in his first scene, and give the actor some indications about how he might best deliver his lines. As this scene unfolds and Ross enters with news that Macbeth has been nominated Thane of Cawdor, modern editions indicate many of Macbeth's speeches as asides: no such marker would have been part of the cue-script, and thus the Macbeth actor has to negotiate cues – 'I pray you' or 'aid of use' – to which his speeches are not replies at all, but introverted meditations.

Another example shows a similar disconnect between the cues and the speeches. When Macbeth meets Lady Macbeth after the murder of Duncan in 2.2, it is clear that he is in his own world: his speeches do not follow on from or even seem to register what is said to him. He continues to remember the haunting scene of the sleeping grooms irrespective of Lady Macbeth's attempts to intervene. Here, a gap between cue and speech gives the actor the clue that he is increasingly withdrawn into his own world, sharing the scene's lines with his interlocutor but really speaking to himself. Perhaps this is the equivalent of Freud's suggestive insight into the relationship between the couple as the expression of a single character split into two personages: 'like two disunited parts of a single psychical individuality' (Freud, 137). As so often in the play, here Macbeth seems essentially to be soliloquizing: talking to himself rather than to others. Breaking the play not into the act and scene divisions which are largely relevant to readers, but instead into the cue-scripts that represent the working script in the playhouse, gives *Macbeth* a very different shape. Analysing cue-scripts in Malcolm and Macduff's encounter in Act 4, or in the edgy conversation between Macbeth, Lady Macbeth and Banquo in 3.1 (brilliantly unsettling in Goold's film of his production), can bring out some of the uncertainties, gaps and miscommunications between characters, and reinstate a more tentative idea of character being iterated through, rather than prior to, speech.

Actors' insights II: Modern

Modern actors approach Shakespearean roles in a quite different way from their early modern predecessors: reading the whole script, watching film versions, studying critical accounts and undergoing extensive group rehearsal. Much of what has been written about and for actors working with Shakespeare services the dominant aim of modern British Shakespearean performance as practised at the Royal Shakespeare Company based in Stratford-on-Avon. This dramatic culture has been summarized by the director John Barton as 'the importance of asking the question 'What is my intention?' If we had to reduce our modern [acting] tradition to one single point I think it would be this' (Barton, 9).

Patsy Rodenburg, voice coach at the RSC, has two useful exercises we might apply here. The first is a series of questions she suggests that the actor should ask about any speech he or she is about to undertake, and the questions are relevant to us for getting a feel for Shakespeare's language use:

- Is the language formal or informal?

- Is the language direct or indirect?

- Does the character use imagery?

- Is the language concrete, full of very specific details?

- Is the language verbose or overblown?

- Does he use analogy or academic references?

- Does the character use more short than long words?

- Does the character enjoy discussion and debate?

- Where does she feel safe in language, where in jeopardy? (Rodenburg 1988: 207–8)

Some of these are difficult to ascertain, but let's try to gloss them.

Signs of informality might include everyday language or imagery, a preponderance of monosyllabic words, a preference for 'thou' rather than 'you', a tendency to abbreviate words (indicated with an apostrophe) and a more broken or shared verse line. Informal lines may follow conventional word order rather than inverting the syntax for metrical effect, and are more likely to run across the line-end (a technique known as enjambment) and thus less likely to end with a piece of punctuation. Conversely, formal language may be polysyllabic, relating to elevated or abstracted or classical ideas, using the verse line as a more closed discipline, preferring 'you': thus, further from everyday speech in terms of register and syntax (the courtly exchange between Duncan and Macbeth in 1.4 is a good example of this form). Indirect language may use abstract nouns or euphemistic or circumlocutory forms of speech, or disturb more colloquial word order; direct language is more likely to be grounded in the here and now of deixis ('there', 'this') or specific props or material objects. Imagery involves similes (something is like something else, such as 'look like th'innocent flower/ But be the serpent under it' (1.5.64–5)) or metaphor (something is something else, such as 'It is a tale/ Told by an idiot, full of sound and fury' (5.5.26–7). Judging whether the language is verbose or overblown can be tricky: often much of Shakespeare's language seems to us to be so. But you should trust your instincts: when the language is difficult to follow or seems repetitive, that is probably for a reason. Short versus long words is self-explanatory. Signs of debate or discussion might be 'yet' or 'but' – verbal indications of a change of argumentative direction – sometimes broken or interrupted syntax indicates thoughts breaking in. Feeling safe in language is another intuitive question: often words or phrases which are difficult to say, perhaps because of a cluster of alliteration, or an unfamiliar polysyllabic word, are indications of lack of verbal security.

Let's take Lady Macbeth's speech in 1.5 and work through Rodenburg's checklist.

Glamis thou art, and Cawdor; and shalt be
What thou art promis'd. – Yet do I fear thy nature:
It is too full o' th' milk of human kindness,
To catch the nearest way. Thou wouldst be great;
Art not without ambition, but without
The illness should attend it: what thou wouldst highly,
That wouldst thou holily; wouldst not play false,
And yet wouldst wrongly win; thou'dst have, great
    Glamis,
That which cries 'Thus thou must do', if thou have it;
And that which rather thou dost fear to do,
Than wishest should be undone. Hie thee hither,
That I may pour my spirits in thine ear;
And chastise with the valour of my tongue
All that impedes thee from the golden round,

> Which fate and metaphysical aid doth seem
> To have thee crown'd withal. (1.5.14–29)

Things to point out here might be the features of informal language: elisions, the use of the intimate 'thou' to address the absent Macbeth, alongside more formal features – syntactical inversion in the opening lines for emphasis, for instance, and the metaphor of the 'milk of human kindness'. Monosyllabic, compressed words dominate, placing particular emphasis on the unusual longer words such as 'ambition' and 'metaphysical'. We might read signs of strain in the tongue-twister quality of 'wouldst and 'thou'dst': the clusters of consonants are sticky in the mouth and slow the speech down. Repetitions and syntactic complexity suggest mental effort as the speaker wrestles with the language just as she wrestles with the ideas it conveys. The rhythm of the words seems to flow more easily in the second half of the speech. The speech comprises two long sentences: the multiple clauses of the first make repeated use of 'but' and 'yet', signalling a kind of mental argument, but this seems to resolve itself with the decisive opening clause of the second sentence: 'Hie thee hither'.

Rodenburg's next exercise develops the interrogative, or questioning, aspect of Shakespeare's longer speeches. She suggests this:

- Look at a whole speech. Count the number of thoughts. Generally there will be between three and five. If more, the character might be unsure or emotionally hesitant. If less, they are very sure and emotionally charged.

- Observe where the thoughts start. Thoughts that begin mid-line are often a sign of unease or instability in the character's processes.

- Notice how long thoughts have more emotional flow, while shorter thoughts are relatively hard and tight.

- Speak the speech actively, linking thought to thought. Experience the power of the bridges and connections between each thought.

- You can do this sitting opposite a partner, and gently pushing, hand to hand, to help you feel each thought connect and intensify.

- Now walk the whole speech, changing direction on each thought.

- When these turns are in your body, change directions within the thought [. . .] Each stage and each turn will add more texture to the thoughts and the voice.

- You will notice how the structure moves a character towards a resolution. They rarely stand still in their thinking. They are always changing as they speak. (Rodenburg 2002: 131–2)

Applying this technique to Lady Macbeth's speech above can flesh out or physicalize the linguistic features we have been discussing. These approaches aren't necessarily comfortable for everyone – some are more at ease with the plays as verbal poetry than as physical embodiment – but they bring the play to its feet in a way that can be active and enlivening.

The language of character: Macbeth and Lady Macbeth

Part of what is clear from Holinshed (see Chapter Two) is that the relationship between Macbeth and Lady Macbeth is unique to Shakespeare's own imagination. There is no suggestion of this strong relationship in Shakespeare's source, in which all we learn of Macbeth's wife is that she 'lay sore upon him to attempt the thing, as she that was very ambitious, burning in unquenchable desire to bear the name of a queen'. From this, Shakespeare conjures a powerful sense of reciprocal encouragement – what psychologists might call a *folie a deux*, or shared delusion.

It's striking to reflect that Shakespeare's plays very rarely focus on married couples. Comedies dramatize courtship rituals and typically end as married life begins, with the dance of the couples at the end of *Much Ado About Nothing* or the entrance of the goddess of marriage, Hymen, to the forest in *As You Like It*, for instance. Shakespeare's tragedies tend to give us widows or widowers, focusing, as in *King Lear* and *Coriolanus,* on relationships between parents and children, particularly between fathers and daughters. But part of Shakespeare's experiment in *Macbeth* seems to have been to show a mature, mutual relationship between husband and wife. As Bradley identifies, the couple 'have no separate ambitions', and, further: 'strange and almost ludicrous as the statement may sound, [Lady Macbeth] is, up to her light, a perfect wife' (Bradley, 316). The play enacts a kind of reverse comedy, a de-courtship, as it traces the different and divergent ways in which the Macbeths respond to their burden of guilt.

This relationship is, like everything else in the play, constructed and conveyed linguistically. Much as the play encourages to speculate about extra-dramatic elements of their characters, all we have to go on is the words that they speak. And their joint scenes are an important skeletal structure for the play as a whole. As Emrys Jones points out, *Macbeth* 'has very few elaborate ensemble scenes: duologues abound' (Jones, 193). Two-handed scenes, such as the debate between Malcolm and Macduff about the attributes of kingship in Act 4, or the edgy interview between Lennox and an unnamed 'Lord' in 3.6, or Banquo and Macbeth's night-time meeting in 2.1 give the play its characteristic small-scale, human dimension. This is a private, rather than a ceremonial world, in which human relations are the building-blocks of social and political life. Crucial among these is the particular dramaturgy of the scenes between Macbeth and Lady Macbeth in 1.5, 1.7, 2.2, 2.3, 3.2 and 3.4. The relationship between husband and wife dominates the anticipation, commission and immediate aftermath of the king's murder. It fades out entirely after the scene in which the ghost of Banquo appears at the feast. As Macbeth tells his wife, 'Strange things I have in head, that will to hand,/ Which must be acted, ere they may be scann'd' (3.4.138–9), the isolation of these former partners of greatness is completed. The couple are never on stage together again, and news of Lady Macbeth's death prompts only the most general of laments on the emptiness of existence, rather than any more feeling recollection of their vital relationship.

Harriet Walter describes the first meeting between Macbeth and Lady Macbeth in 1.5:

When husband and wife first meet on stage, they have no need to spell things out. Macbeth has three lines in the scene. He has paved much of the way in his letter. Although if anyone had intercepted it they would have found nothing incriminating, to Lady Macbeth's fertile ear it reads: 'The way is clear, my dearest partner of greatness, and I know you will know what to do.' All he has to say when he greets her is: 'My dearest love,/ Duncan comes here tonight.' We have already been party to Lady Macbeth's extreme reaction to the same news earlier, and now she can afford a calm 'And when goes hence?' (there is something of a test going on here, as thought she is really asking: 'And is he going to leave here alive, do you think? If not, what are you going to do about it?'). He replies, 'Tomorrow, as he purposes.' So far, so innocent, as if the room were bugged. But why add 'as he purposes'? A simple 'Tomorrow' would have done. In the husband-and-wife telepathy this added phrase means: 'At least that is what he thinks,' and that is enough of a cue for Lady Macbeth to pounce in with: 'O! never/Shall sun that morrow see!'. Then Shakespeare builds two beats of silence into the five-beat line, during which. . . what? It is a truly pregnant pause. Husband and wife search one another's faces. hold their breath in shock. the thoughts

they had dared to think alone are now brought literally face
to face. It is the moment. (Walter, 18)

What Walter identifies here in her interpretation of the encounter is an unspoken, shared ambition. Macbeth's 'as he purposes' gives Lady Macbeth the cue for her 'o never': the pair
are closely in tune on the issue, almost without articulating it.
What is captured in these lines is less that Lady Macbeth is
urging him to something, and more that the couple are working together. The intimacy of their relationship is expressed
physically in Trevor Nunn's television film, where 'Macbeth
caresses her breasts and back. Her voice is soft and low. Rapt
in his pleasure at being with her he answers unthinkingly'
(Kliman, 141). The sense of an erotic chemistry between the
couple has often been presented in such physical terms in the
theatre – as a sensuous equivalent of their interlocking, deeply
mutually aware language in the play.

The next conversation between the couple comes immediately after Macbeth's soliloquy discussed in the previous
chapter. Macbeth's broken-backed image of 'vaulting ambition' that 'falls on th'other' (1.7.28–9) is interrupted by Lady
Macbeth's entrance. For Patsy Rodenburg, this puts the blame
squarely on the woman: 'having considered his own actions in
the perspective of a much larger debate about crime, punishment and cosmic law, Macbeth fails explicitly to conclude that
he won't murder Duncan – and thus leaves himself exposed to
manipulation by his wife. The bridge over the chasm is missing its final section – Macbeth has been left dangling within
sight of the other side but unable to reach it. This incomplete
architecture is the real tragedy of Macbeth. He kills Duncan
knowing he shouldn't' (Rodenburg 2002: 137–8). On the
other hand, we could argue that Macbeth's speech is already
falling into incoherence when Lady Macbeth enters, and thus
it is cognitively unlikely that he would conclude not to murder
Duncan: the final lines of his soliloquy are not obviously leading towards a particular conclusion.

What particular words or phrases signify is not something we can always determine from reading them on the page. Intonation is crucial to establishing the meaning given to specific lines by specific performers. Take, for instance, the exchange between Macbeth and Lady Macbeth after her allusion to the 'babe that milks me' (1.7.55) whose brains she would dash out, 'had I so sworn/ As you have done to this' (1.7.58–9):

MACBETH If we should fail?
LADY MACBETH We fail? (1.7.59–60)

The pointing here is from the Folio text, but then, as now, a question mark was an equivocal piece of punctuation. In early modern printing it could be used either to indicate a question or an exclamation mark (the equivalent mark in modern printing would be!); in modern usage the increasing frequency of what's called 'uptalk' (or more technically high-rise terminals), the habit of ending sentences with a rising intonation tone that suggests a question even where it is a statement, might be the aural equivalent of this ambiguous punctuation.

The great Romantic actress Sarah Siddons first played Lady Macbeth in 1785, and the part became indelibly associated with her. Even modern actors approaching the role often refer back to her much-reported performance. A contemporary critic Anna Jameson described her approach to 'we fail': 'Mrs. Siddons adopted successively three different intonations in giving the words we fail. At first as a quick contemptuous interrogation. Afterwards with the note of admiration, and an accent of indignant astonishment, laying the emphasis on 'we'. Lastly, she fixed on what I am convinced is the true reading – we fail. With the simple period, modulating her voice to a deep, low, resolute tone, which settled the issue at once – as though she had said, 'If we fail, why then we fail, and all is over.' This is consistent with the dark fatalism of the character, and the sense of the line following – and the effect was sublime, almost awful' (Furness, 80).

The question of how Lady Macbeth delivers 'we fail?' and how editors direct or permit different readings is a perennial one. Eighteenth-century editors were unconvinced that Lady Macbeth could be asking a genuine question and so tended to emend the question mark into an exclamation mark. One suggested 'she admits a possibility of miscarriage, but at the same instant shows herself not afraid of the result. Her answer, therefore, communicates no discouragement to her husband'. Sometimes a full stop was preferred: 'we prefer the quiet self-possession of the punctuation we have adopted' (Furness, 80). Modern editions tend to retain the question mark while acknowledging its blurred usage in the early modern period. As Sian Thomas, Lady Macbeth in a production directed Dominic Cooke in 2004 observes:

> There are so many ways of saying these two monosyllables, with such different worlds of implication: it can be a question, either suddenly apprehensive about the possibility of failure or completely dismissing the very idea ('We . . . fail?' or 'We fail?!', or 'We, fail???') or it can be a quick fatalistic shrug, or all sorts of shades in between. (Dobson, 96)

What is also clear is that the two words stand alone on a line. Some interpreters of incomplete lines in Shakespeare's plays suggest that they script a specific length of pause that would fill out the line to the usual rhythm. If that is the case here, Lady Macbeth's question is followed by a lengthy, four-beat pause: another gap for interpretation. Is the pause a sign of her resolution and strength – almost daring Macbeth to contradict her – or of doubt and hesitation? Thus, 'We fail' stands almost as a verbal equivalent to Lady Macbeth's fainting fit as the murder of Duncan is discovered: is this a 'genuine', or strategic, diversion from her husband's hyperbolic speech of exculpation about his murder of the grooms of Duncan's bedchamber: ' help me hence, ho!' On both occasions, the only possible answer is always a contingent one in a specific performance.

The scene of the aftermath of the murder shows how the couple's reactions to what they have done differ. Lady Macbeth enters first: 'That which hath made them drunk, hath made me bold' (2.2.1): eight lines consisting almost entirely of monosyllables. The suggestion, writes Patsy Rodenburg, 'is of intoxication, and the tight hold is typical of someone, even slightly drunk, focusing to stay in control' (Rodenburg 2002: 71). The speech is interrupted by a noise – 'it was the owl that shrieked' – and the edgy suggestion of the fearful noises of discovery haunts the spiky dialogue. Macbeth's entry – 'who's there? – What, ho?' (2.2.8) – introduces a strain of questions. There are around about 16 in the scene (different editions may punctuate differently, see Chapter One): Lady Macbeth has only four of them, and hers are more practical than her husband's panicky interrogations: 'what do you mean?' (2.2.39); 'why did you bring these daggers from the place?' (2.2.47).

Looking at this scene in an edition of collected works, rather than a single playtext that has a lot of explanatory notes on the page, means that more of the text fits on a single opening and we can see at a glance the shape it makes on the page. Here we have longer speeches by Lady Macbeth and shorter fragments by her husband: the broken lines make the speech jagged on the page and 'create pauses, holes in the vigour of the scene' (Rodenburg 2002: 371). This rough-textured speech captures the edgy, nervous atmosphere in the immediate aftermath of the murder of Duncan. It also shows us how the couple are drawing apart. The analysis of cue-lines above made clear that Macbeth's speeches in this scene, dwelling on the fate of the grooms, follow on from Lady Macbeth's cues but do not in any sense respond to them. Her urging 'these deeds must not be thought' (2.2.32), for example, entirely fails to interrupt Macbeth thinking obsessively on these deeds, as he replies 'Methought I heard a voice cry "Sleep no more"' (2.2.34–5), repeating his inability to 'pronounce 'Amen' four times in seven lines. Questions are answered with other questions: 'Did you not speak? When?' (2.2.16): all is choppy, dull of doubt.

Line 16, with its pentameter strung across 4 short speeches, encapsulates the scene's pervading jumpiness and strung-out tension.

> Did you not speak?
> > When?
> > > Now.
> > > > As I descended? (2.2.16)

Some editions add Lady Macbeth's 'Ay' (2.2.17) as a final syllable to this extended line (the Folio does not indicate through the indentation common in modern editions that the separate speeches might contribute to a shared line, so does not help us here). Working with actors to bring out the scene's emotional temperature, however, voice coach Patsy Rodenburg prefers the scripted pause that might be indicated by an incomplete line: 'There follows a remarkable exchange: Lady Macbeth's "Ay" – four beat pause – and Macbeth's Hark – four beat pause. Shakespeare is doing in verse and silence what Hitchcock did with music and camera angles: creating enormous suspense and tension' (Rodenburg 2002: 372). Rodenburg's cinematic simile here can be visualized in Orson Welles' film. Long takes stress the tense dynamic between the couple. Often in their conversations Macbeth faces towards the camera and Lady Macbeth stands behind him, so that her taunts leave their mark on his expression. The backdrop is the crazy, expressionist castle in chiaroscuro, dwarfing the protagonists. Welles' soundscape is the gothic track of thunder and lightning, implicitly connecting Lady Macbeth with the witches.

Rodenburg also points out that Lady Macbeth's diction here mostly relates to action and practicalities: what has happened, what needs to be done to cover their crime. She focuses on specific objects and concrete nouns: possets, owls, crickets, daggers. Macbeth, by contrast, inhabits a different reality: 'The voices he hears are what's real to him. His anchoring is in prayers, God, sleep, death, life, minds, nature, oceans' (Rodenburg 2002: 376). Lady Macbeth is pragmatic, calm: 'A little water clears us of this deed' (2.2.66); Macbeth's mind races into symbolism: 'wake Duncan with thy knocking' (2.2.73). These different linguistic patterns correspond to an increasing gap between the couple, a gap that will open out as the play unfolds.

The language of the play

A different approach, however, derives from understanding the language of the play as creating the characters, rather than the other way around. Characters in Shakespeare do not pre-exist their speeches (as real people do); rather, they are conjured out of the spoken words. It is part of the skill of the characterization to make us think the characters pre-exist their words and there is a person speaking, rather than being spoken. Speech comes before character in a play. Some characters are functional rather than psychological: think of the Old Man, or Lennox, or Ross, for instance, whose roles in the play are choric or representative, rather than psychological: these are commentators rather than distinct individuals. That said, an actor playing the part would probably want to argue for something more sustained and interior in terms of motivation, and some productions amplify his part considerably to aid this. In Polanski's film, for example, Ross is a treacherous double-dealer, affecting to warn Lady Macduff before leading the assault on the castle, and then feigning grief as he reports the murders to Macduff, adding together his equivocal placement in the film to disturbing effect.

Just as some characters may seem to be roles rather than people, so too some speeches seem to be for the benefit of the play than the character: it doesn't really make sense, as

Graham Bradshaw identifies, to interpret Macbeth's 'The multitudinous scenes incarnadine/ Making the green one red' (2.2.61–2) with 'this character is a secret reader with a tremendous vocabulary who is thoughtful enough to provide a monosyllabic gloss for the less well educated': the speech here 'belongs to the representation but not to the character' (Kliman, 59) or, to put it another way, it, unlike the character, knows we are at the theatre. We might say something similar about the play's use of rhyme. The 'blank' in 'blank verse', the term given to the rhythmic lines of Shakespeare and his contemporary dramatists, means unrhymed. Whereas earlier drama had made use of rhyme, blank verse had instead a skeleton of stressed syllables. Rhyme in Shakespeare's earlier plays was relatively common, but here in *Macbeth* rhyme sounds unnatural and glib. Sometimes it may be used as if the characters are consciously themselves rhyming: one television version of the play shows the relationship between Macbeth and his wife by showing that they 'are accustomed, evidently, to talking to each other in clichés, for after he is settled on murder, he recites the final couplet of the scene accompanied by her sotto voce echoes and her nods of the head in unison, "Away and mock the time with fairest show:/ False heart must hide what the false heart doth know" (1.7.82–3)' (Kliman, 103). Here the rhyme imposes its own inevitability on the decided action, putting its linguistic weight behind what has been decided. But when Siward speaks to the soldiers at the end of 5.4, the rhymes seem vacuous and over-emphatic:

> The time approaches,
> That will with due decision make us know
> What we shall say we have, and what we owe;
> Thoughts speculative their unsure hopes relate,
> But certain issue, strokes must arbitrate;
> Towards which advance the war. (5.4.16–21)

It's a strange speech: anti-climactic, curiously unclear, with its sequence of monosyllables echoing earlier soliloquies by the

Macbeths. The heavy rhymes may suggest the 'marching' stage direction, but they also make the speech seem dubious. 'Owe', 'speculative' and 'unsure' all suggest moral uncertainty. Badly written, or part of the slightly underwhelming characterization of the English forces? Or, to put it another way, is this Siward or the play speaking? 'I doubt', wrote A. C. Bradley, 'if any other great play of Shakespeare's contains so many speeches which a student of the play, if they were quoted to him, would be puzzled to assign to the speakers [. . .] We may almost say [it] is simply Shakespeare's writing, not that of Shakespeare become another person' (Bradley, 326).

Further, the play has its own idiolect: a shared poetry in which speeches echo each other rather as a musical motif might be taken up by different instruments in a jazz band or orchestra. Echoes, running similes, interrelated metaphors, serve less to individuate particular speakers and more to integrate a poetic whole. For example, Lady Macbeth's awful recognition in her sleepwalking 'what's done, cannot be undone' (5.1.) recalls to us Macbeth' soliloquy 'if it were done when 'tis done', but it does so poetically rather than realistically (she did not hear it, but we did). That's to say part of its dramatic purpose at the beginning of Act 5 is to recap for us the soundscape of the play thus far, to loop back to the feverish, fraught period around Duncan's murder, just before the play approaches its final sequence. In this sense its meaning is dramaturgical rather than psychological: it is a product of the play rather than the individual.

At their simplest, these connective verbal structures are aural rather than referential – it is the sounds of words rather than their meanings that are fused together. As in Lady Macbeth's speech above, we might begin to distinguish the syllable 'done' as a past participle but as also immanent in 'dunnest', 'Duncan' and 'Dunsinane' – over 60 cumulative occurrences – or the cluster of 'kin' sounds in words including 'kinsman', king', 'enkindle', 'kindness'. Heard in this way – and it is worth remembering that the experience of theatre was a largely aural one for early modern audiences (the word means 'hearers') – the knocking at the porters' gate becomes an ironic reinforcement of the irrevocable fact of Duncan's murder. 'Wake Duncan with thy knocking: I wouldst thou couldst' (2.2.73). The past tense Dun/done and the mocking whisper of 'no king' in 'knocking' dance subliminally. In his famous short essay 'On the knocking at the gate in *Macbeth*' (1823) the romantic essayist Thomas de Quincey, best known for his *Confessions of an English Opium-Eater* (1821) argued that the repeated knocking was affecting because it directed attention away from Duncan towards Macbeth: 'Murder in ordinary cases, where the sympathy is wholly directed to the case of the murdered person, is an incident of coarse and vulgar horror' whereas 'in the murderer, such a murderer as a poet will condescend to, there must be raging some great storm of passion, – jealousy, ambition, vengeance, hatred, – which will create a hell within him; and into this hell we are to look.' For de Quincey the murder of Duncan takes place in an 'awful parenthesis' suspending everyday life: the knocking signals 'the re-establishment of the goings-on of the world in which we live', where 'the human has made its reflux on the fiendish: the pulses of life are beginning to beat again' (De Quincey, 93).

But the echo of 'king' in the repeated word 'knocking' (4 times in 20 lines at the end of 2.2) may suggest that Duncan is half-remembered as a verbal ghost. The word 'king' throughout is freighted with significance. Discussing the witches' prophecy in Act 1, 'All hail Macbeth! that shalt be King hereafter' (1.3.50), Derek Jacobi recalls his own interpretation: 'Macbeth's response to the witches' greeting is hesitant and interrogative. He considers the idea, the pause I used on the word king in 'to be king/ Stands not within the prospect of belief' [1.3.73–4] seeming to hold it up for momentary examination' (Jacobi, 197). Lady Macbeth has overleapt herself when she responds to the messenger's 'The king comes here to-night' with 'Thou'rt mad to say it' (1.5.30): momentarily, she interprets the word 'King' as referring to Macbeth himself, because she has been daydreaming about his future success. The word can never be neutral. Apart from Macbeth himself, no one ever names him king: the word is reserved for Duncan and, in 4.3, the English king, and otherwise deridingly used as the suffix to verbs of continuous action – 'sticking', 'leave-taking', 'shaking'. A single stage direction in the Folio text grudgingly allows 'Macbeth as King' (3.4), but the formulation rather undermines his claim to the title rather than endorsing it – to be 'as' King is not quite to be King. The faint echo in speech 'life's but a walking shadow' (5.5.24) may indicate how far he has fallen. Only when Malcolm enters to claim the kingdom does the derogated word 'king' return, three times in as many lines, to establish his right, where the repeated 'Hail King' recalls, and perhaps rehabilitates, the witches' triple greeting in Act 1.

These echoes of verbal patterns give the play a particular texture in which language has a non-referential aspect: what is important here, as in the puns and wordplay so beloved of the early modern period, is less what words mean than how they sound. To use the vocabulary of semiotics, which distinguishes between the signifier – the word – and the signified – the real-world thing that it denotes, these forms of poetic patterning draw on relationships between signifiers. Or to put it a different way, borrowing from the American modernist poet Archibald MacLeish, 'A poem should not mean/ But be' ('Ars Poetica', 1926).

Image clusters

Perhaps more recognizable to modern readers are patterns of imagery and association, where the links are between signifieds. One of the play's dominant image clusters is that of clothing. Explicit references to the disparity between the office and the man are figured as ill-fitting or inappropriate clothing, sometimes visualized in performance. Laurence Olivier's crown was too big for him throughout the 1955 production directed by Glen Byam Shaw at Stratford-upon-Avon. 'Why do you dress me/ In borrow'd robes?' (1.4.108–9) asks Macbeth, when he is given the title of a man he knows to be still living, a 'prosperous gentleman' (1.4.73), and he develops the imagery as he tries to resist Lady Macbeth's implacable resolve: 'I have bought/ Golden opinions from all sorts of people,/ Which would be worn now in their newest gloss,/ Not cast aside so soon' (1.7.31–4). Lady Macbeth picks up the threat: 'Was the hope drunk/ Wherein you dressed yourself?' (1.7.35–6). But others use the same trope. Banquo explains Macbeth's distraction: 'New honours come upon him/ Like our strange garments, cleave not to their mould/ But with the aid of use' (1.3.145–7). When, in the final act, hitherto unknown thanes in Malcolm's army deploy the same metaphor – 'He cannot buckle his distemper'd cause/ Within the belt of rule' (5.2.15–16); 'now does he feel his title/ Hang loose about him, like a giant's robe/ Upon a dwarfish thief' (5.2.20–2) – we can recognize that this is less a figure of speech of individual characters and their world-view and more a poetic device of the play's total idiolect.

Explicit uses of the imagery help activate more submerged elements of the pattern. Macbeth's extraordinary action in dispatching Macdonwald, reported in 1.2, is described in the unusual negative 'unseam'd' (1.2.22) – a kind of anti-stitching, ripping rather than mending the fabric of the body. The grooms' daggers are said to be 'unmannerly breech'd with gore' (2.3.114): the image here is of being clothed in breeches (or perhaps since 'unmannerly', unbreeched), the blood as a grotesquely sticky garment on their weapons. Lady Macbeth's 'blanket' (1.5.52, discussed in Chapter One as part of the analysis of the play's domestic language) and, in the same speech, 'pall' (1.5.50) or shroud, clothing for the dead or the lament for sleep that 'knits up the ravell'd sleave of care' (2.2.36) – a homely image of darning as a way to bind up the day's concerns in rest – these all develop the textile metaphor, in part to contribute to the play's horrifically distorted lexis of domesticity.

Other image clusters can be traced through the play. Macbeth is a play suffused with darkness. Remarkably, for a

play apparently performed in the open air, daylit Globe theatre, it creates a sustained atmosphere of gathering shadows.
The witches' chant 'Fair is foul and foul is fair,/ Hover through
the fog and filthy air' (1.1.11–12) establishes the murkiness as
physical and spiritual, rather as Orson Welles' film of 1948,
shot in atmospheric black and white, views the entire story
through swirling fog and shadows. 'Light thickens' (3.2.50):
the word 'thick' has contradictory associations of slowness
and constriction, as well as, in the common coupling 'thick
and fast', of expedition and haste. (*OED* 5b 'occurring in
quick succession; rapid, frequent'). Darkness and movement
or speed (as discussed in Chapter Two), are thus connected.

Banquo designates the witches 'instruments of Darkness'
(1.4.124), and Lady Macbeth is connected to them by her
invocation 'come, thick Night,/ And pall thee in the dunnest smoke of Hell,/ That my keen knife see not the wound
it makes,/ Nor Heaven peep through the blanket of the
dark' (1.5.49–52). Darkness here is summoned as a kind of
anaesthetic or disguise, preventing both the agent of wickedness – my keen knife – and an external judge – Heaven –
from spying on human action. Many of the play's scenes take
place at night and for the early modern theatre this lighting
effect is indicated primarily verbally, supported by the visual
device of torches onstage. When Duncan arrives at Dunsinane
the stage direction in the Folio text calls for 'Torches', even
though the following speeches, about the delicate air and the
'temple-haunting martlet' (1.6.4), suggest daytime. Bradley
identifies this scene as one of only two occurrences of sun-
shine in the play: his other example is 'when at the close the
avenging army gathers to rid the earth of its shame' (Bradley,
279). 'Torches' are also indicated at the opening of 1.7 and
2.1, which takes place after midnight under a starless sky:
'There's husbandry in heaven;/ Their candles are all out'
(2.1.4–5). Banquo and Fleance are again in the dark for the
scene of Banquo's murder, just after sunset: 'The west yet
glimmers with some streaks of day' (3.3.5). The confusion
of the ensuing scuffle is emphasized by the repeated calls for

'light' as Banquo tries to save himself and his son. Macbeth
has predicted that 'Good things of Day begin to droop and
drowse/ Whiles Night's black agents to their preys do rouse'
(3.2.52–3). Ross reports that after the murder of the king 'by
th'clock 'tis day,/ And yet dark night strangles the travelling
lamp' (2.4.6–7). Such darkness is dangerous: 'men must not
walk too late' (3.6.7). Sleepless nights signal the disruption
in the normal order caused by regicide. Lady Macbeth carries 'a Taper' in her sleepwalking scene, and her gentlewoman
tells the doctor that 'she has light by her continually; 'tis her
command' (5.1.23–4). If, post-murder, Lady Macbeth abjures
the darkness, Macbeth seems to embrace it. 'Come, seeling
Night,/ Scarf up the tender eye of pitiful Day' (3.2.46–7).
After their abortive banquet – presumably another scene lit
by candlelight – and half-way through the play, Macbeth asks
'what is the night?' 'Almost at odds with morning, which is
which' (3.5.125–6). The play's plot, structural and ethical, is
here encapsulated in the struggle between night and day.

The sheer density of verbal reference to darkness in the
play is extreme. It's almost, writes Tony Tanner, 'as though
darkness itself had become a vicious agent in its own right'
(Tanner, 555). Such darkness is, of course, a moral as well
as a physical condition. Ross's question 'Is't night's predomi-
nance, or the day's shame,/ That darkness does the face of
earth entomb' (2.4.8–9) is, for Tanner, 'not only the central
question of this play but of tragedy itself' (Tanner, 555): to put
it another way, does evil happen because of its own strength
or because of the weakness of good? It's a question the play
asks but does not answer. Productions, such as Trevor Nunn's
in 1974, that stress a religious context for the play, in which
Macbeth is guilty of a sacrilege that only the saintly king of
England can help to absolve, have to add to the play to bring
out this Manichean or Christian framework. Nunn set the
scene between Malcolm and Macduff in the choir stalls of a
cathedral in front of a prominent crucifix; Goold also had the
two men meet in a church and emphasized Malcolm's evident
piety against his claims of venality. The idea that the play's

political and ethical trajectory is the passage from darkness to light is repeated. Malcolm's call to arms to the bereft Macduff notes that 'the night is long that never finds the day' (4.3.240): like other of his bland comforts in the scene it is potentially hollow, but, as the balance of power shifts towards him, gains weight. (It also has its literal counterpart in the scene which immediately follows, the long night of Lady Macbeth's sleep-walking, a sickness from which, metaphorically, she never wakes.) Seyward's report to his commander that Dunsinane is surrendered and 'the day almost itself professes yours' (5.7.27) is more than a figure of speech: in the reading of this image cluster, Malcolm has won the day back from the night (compare this with more equivocal interpretations of his final accession, as discussed in Chapter Two).

So, how many children had Lady Macbeth?

In addition to the networks of imagery of darkness and of clothing is another prominent cluster associated with babies. Because this image cluster has so preoccupied critics, it allows us to set a poetic and a psychological reading of the play alongside each other. Working with the poetic clusters I have been identifying has been a tendency of mid-twentieth-century criticism – exemplified in the exhaustive listing of imagery in Caroline Spurgeon's *Shakespeare's Imagery and What it Tells Us*. Critical approaches like Spurgeon's were marked by a retreat from excessively novelistic understandings of the play as driven by character and instead an intense focus on its poetic texture. We might understand this critical backlash under the heading 'How many children had Lady Macbeth?' This question was posed in the title of an essay by L. C. Knights in 1933, and invoked an extensive critical and methodological argument. The foundations of this debate are evident from the text. At 1.7.54–5, Lady Macbeth states: 'I have given suck, and

know/ How tender 'tis to love the babe that milks me'. But no
child appears in the play, and Macbeth clearly distinguishes
himself from Banquo when he recalls that the witches:

> hail'd him father to a line of kings:
> Upon my head they plac'd a fruitless crown,
> And put a barren sceptre in my gripe,
> Thence to be wrench'd with an unlineal hand
> No son of mine succeeding. (3.1.59–63)

This might mean that the child was a daughter, but the absence
of any Macbeth offspring in the play is striking, and it may
be that Macduff confirms this on the devastating news of his
family's murder: 'He has no children' (4.3.216): the alternative reading is that he refers to Malcolm at this point.

Knights' essay 'How many children had Lady Macbeth?'
was intended as an explicit riposte to Bradley's highly influential character criticism. To be fair to Bradley on the specific point of Lady Macbeth's children, it is not an issue he
spends much time discussing, and he is concerned about it
in relation to Macbeth's own fears about the succession and
the meaning of Macduff's 'he has no children', rather than
Lady Macbeth's psychology. But Knights correctly observes
that Bradley, heir to the realist novel-reading culture of late
Victorian England, works on the assumption that 'the most
profitable discussion of Shakespeare's tragedies is in terms
of the characters of which they are composed' (Knights, 15).
Consider Bradley's summary of Macbeth: 'he was exceed-
ingly ambitious. He must have been so by temper. The tendency must have been greatly strengthened by his marriage'
(Bradley, 294) whereas 'character', for Knights, is 'brought
into being by written or spoken words'. 'A Shakespeare play
is a dramatic poem' (Knights, 16), and therefore we should
focus on Shakespeare's 'use of language to obtain a total complex emotional response' (Knights, 18). Knights never actually
addresses the question of Lady Macbeth's children, other than
to imply that the answer cannot be found in an investigation

of her character: his famous title actually misrepresents his concerns in the essay.

Taking up Knights' invitation to see the play as a total poem, we can begin to see that Lady Macbeth's imaginary infant functions within a metaphorical economy heavily invested in images of children. From 'Pity, like a naked new-born babe' (1.7.21) to 'bring forth men-children only' (1.7.73), from the focus on Banquo's son Fleance and the chirpy young Macduff, and from the 'bloody child' and 'child crowned' of the witches' infernal apparitions (4.1.76SD; 86SD) to the image of Macduff, invincible since he was 'from his mother's womb/ Untimely ripp'd' (5.8.15–16), the play is haunted by children. Macbeth describes the thanes as 'children' to their father/ king Duncan (1.4.25); Hecate in turn describes him as 'a way-ward son' (3.5.11) the word 'wayward' is close to the term 'weyard' or 'weyward' used of the witches, as discussed in Chapter One). Macbeth vows to exterminate Macduff's children using the imagery of firstborn: 'From this moment/ The very firstlings of my heart shall be/ The firstlings of my hand' (4.1.146–8). Simon Palfrey identifies the 'alarming connection in the repetition between the act of thinking and infanticide' (Palfrey, 59). Productions often amplify this verbal and visual preoccupation. One review of Michael Boyd's 2011 produc-tion for the Royal Shakespeare Company records: 'His most striking device is to have the weird sisters played by children, first revealed suspended in the air as if they had been hanged. It is a truly shocking moment that makes the skin crawl. Later these ghostly prophetic infants reappear as Macduff's inno-cent children, harrowingly butchered by Macbeth's thugs in a scene that is almost too harrowing to watch.' Adrian Noble in 1986 made 'effective play with the running theme of chil-dren as symbols of innocence and promise. At the start the witches rescue a small boy from the battlefield. Fleance sits on the throne, after Macbeth has been crowned, in a cheeky reminder of the future. Most effectively of all, Macbeth plays blind man's buff on the heath with three laughing, pretty chil-dren summoned by the witches to circle endlessly around him;

it is a vision of a future that belongs to Banquo' (O'Connor, 677). Ron Daniels' 1999 production in New York had the witches give birth to the apparitions; Macbeth in Penny Woolcock's television *Macbeth on the Estate* encounters three creepily knowing children as the witches in a den decorated with candles, mirrors and other detritus.

These are all interpolations to Shakespeare's text, just as he himself had added the references to children to his own source material. But if we look at again at Holinshed we can see that he has also left out some material on this topic. Shakespeare combines the story of Macbeth's accession to the throne with that of the murder of a previous monarch, King Duff, at whose death nature was disordered: 'Monstrous sights also that were seen within the Scottish kingdom that year were these: horses in Louthian, being of singular beauty and swiftness, did eat their own flesh, and would in no wise taste any other meat. In Angus there was a gentlewoman brought forth a child without eyes, nose, hand, or foot. There was a sparrowhawk also strangled by an owl. Neither was it any less wonder that the sun, as before is said, was continually covered with clouds for six months space.' The influence of this passage on the conversation between the Old Man and Ross in 2.4 is clear: 'By th'clock 'tis day,/ And yet dark night strangles the travelling lamp'; 'A falcon tow'ring in her pride of place/ Was by a mousing owl hawked at, and killed', Duncan's horses 'ate each other' 'to th'amazement of mine eyes' (2.4.6–7, 12–13, 18–19). The one element of this disruption that is left out is what the marginal note to Holinshed signals 'a monstrous child'. Perhaps this suggests that children are not in the play, as they are in the source and in contemporary pamphlets, potentially monstrous portents of wickedness: they are an innocent alternative to rather than a corrupted symptom of, the play's evil.

Understanding why this child imagery is so prevalent is a more difficult question – and perhaps not an entirely necessary interpretative procedure. (We can only really know that it is there: the why is inevitably speculative.) But there are different approaches that might shine some light. We might try to understand this imagery by reference to Shakespeare's source: the wife of Macbeth has a child by a previous marriage, an infant who is not the offspring of Macbeth. But if that straightforward reason were all we needed, presumably Shakespeare would have provided it. Instead, Shakespeare seems here to have employed one of his characteristic techniques on his source material – what Stephen Greenblatt calls 'strategic opacity' (Greenblatt, 324): Shakespeare's tendency to strip out clear motivations, or relations of cause and effect, where he finds them in his sources. When we see this tactic over and over again (in the motivation of Iago, for instance, in *Othello*, or in the reasons for Hamlet's madness) it comes to look deliberate, a withholding of information precisely to create uncertainty and speculation, as it has done in the case of Lady Macbeth.

We might have a go at placing the cluster of images historically. Marjorie Garber reminds us of 'the dominant figure of King James, whose image is everywhere in Macbeth' (Garber, 697). James I's accession to the English throne ended a period of extreme uncertainty about the Elizabethan succession, and his arrival in London with two sons and a daughter established a reassuring sense of a new royal dynasty. Perhaps the play's fascination with fertility and sterility, with accession through violence and through birth ('Your children shall be kings.' 'You shall be King' (1.3.86)) reworks this period of historical anxiety in the safe Stuart context. The aftermath of the Gunpowder Plot may also be relevant. In his speech to Parliament in November 1605 just after the conspiracy had been discovered, James recalled an early threat to his life, referring to an attempt to induce a miscarriage in his pregnant mother Mary Queen of Scots, possibly orchestrated by her husband Henry Stuart, Lord Darnley: 'while I was yet in my mothers belly': 'I should have beene baptized in blood'. There may be a suggestion here of the 'bloody child', of Macduff's miraculous birth, and of the repeated fantasies – symbolic and enacted – of violence towards children in the play.

Fraught maternal relations in the play are the corollary of its preoccupation with children. *Macbeth* may be seen to participate in the misogyny that many historians have uncovered as a feature of James' court and which they have tended to understand as a cultural (i.e. male) sigh of relief after almost half a century of female rule. In its witches and the depiction of Lady Macbeth, the play indulges fantasies of monstrous femininity, but even its ideal wife and mother, Lady Macduff, falls victim to its insistent patterns of male violence. In a rightly influential psychoanalytic account, Janet Adelman identifies the play's 'representation of primitive fears about male identity and autonomy itself, about those looming female presences who threaten to control one's actions and one's mind' (Adelman, 131). (That these fears are not securely in the historical past might be suggested by the surprising availability of Lady Macbeth now as a stereotype of any woman powerful in the public sphere – Hillary Clinton, for example, or Cherie Booth, wife of the former British prime minister Tony Blair, who was dubbed by the newspapers 'Lady McBlair'.) In the end, Macduff is able to defeat Macbeth because in two important ways he is distinct from female influence: he has abandoned his wife and children, and he has been 'from his mother's womb/ Untimely ripp'd' (5.8.15–16), or born by cesarian section (almost inevitably fatal for the mother in this period). The debate in the play about what signifies proper maleness ultimately seems to enforce Lady Macbeth's rather savage view: 'When you durst do it, then you were a man' (1.7.49): to be properly masculine is to be violent, and victims of this violence are thus implicitly feminized, like Duncan, compared to the rape victim Lucrece. This may work particularly in a historical context eager to separate itself from the reign of Queen Elizabeth and for James, too, psychically to rid himself of his own mother, Mary Queen of Scots, who had been executed for treason (it's sometimes suggested that the apparition of the line of Scottish kings from Banquo to, implicitly, James, in 4.1 works numerically only if Mary Stuart is airbrushed out of this patrilinear chimera).

The ending of the play, in which a patriarchal coalition of fathers and sons converges on Dunsinane bearing symbolically regenerative green boughs, and where Lady Macbeth is despatched offstage and the witches are seemingly forgotten entirely, thus serves as a fiction of male parthenogenesis or self-birth: what Adelman calls 'the excision of maternal origin' (Adelman, 146) that is part of the psychological terrain of Freudian notions of the self.

But we might also work to understand the images as components not of psychology or history but of poetry. Cleanth Brooks asks why the image of pity as a 'naked new-born babe' occurs to Macbeth, given that it is 'odd, to say the least. Is the babe natural or supernatural – an ordinary, helpless baby, who, as newborn, could not, of course, even toddle, still less stride the blast? Or is it some infant Hercules, quite capable of striding the blast, but, since it is powerful and not helpless, hardly the typical pitiable object?' (Wain, 184). For Brooks this paradox is resolved because the image of the child is an image of the future, and 'all those enlarging purposes which make life meaningful, and it symbolizes, furthermore, all those emotional and – to Lady Macbeth – irrational ties which make a man more than a machine – which render him human' (Wain, 198). The logic of the repeatedly invoked or embodied child in this analysis, then, is that it must always be destroyed, as the taunting image of the humanity from which the regicide Macbeth has forever exiled himself.

It's no accident that both Knights and Brooks call *Macbeth* a poem, for they bring to bear the techniques of analysis that each had honed on their study of poetry. As Nicholas Brooke notes, Lady Macbeth's baby 'takes its place, with Macbeth's naked new-born babe, and all the other babes of the play, in a dimension well beyond the reach of the characters'. Brooke adds: 'I do not believe that that example need be any special problem to the actress' (Brooke, 14). But actors and directors themselves seem to have taken a consistently different view on this question. 'How many children had Lady Macbeth?' may have become a rhetorical nod to a certain academic

methodology, but for theatre practitioners it has none of the
archness it does in contemporary scholarship. Harriet Walter,
preparing her performance of Lady Macbeth, describes how
she read with incredulity an academic footnote dismissing as
irrelevant the question of her character's children: for a performer, the issue is vital. Indeed, many modern productions
of the play have made the absent Macbeth child a powerful
emotional centre of the play.

Walter outlines the thinking of Doran's production, which
believed the Macbeths had had a child who died.

> This seemed to us the most likely and contained the riches
> theatrical juice. But how, I protested, could a woman who
> knows 'How tender 'tis to love the babe that milks me,'
> and has seen that baby die, even contemplate the thought
> of dashing an infant's brains out? I had fallen into the trap
> of seeing this violent image as proof of Lady Macbeth's
> heartlessness. But once I started to act the scene and feel
> the desperate energy of it, I understood that the opposite
> was the case. Lady Macbeth is thinking up the supreme,
> most horrendous sacrifice imaginable to her in order to
> shame her husband into keeping his pledge. She never has
> to match deeds to her word, but to dare to speak such pain-
> laden words is in itself impressive. (Walter, 31)

The recent theatrical tradition of the Macbeths as bereaved
parents has thus reanimated the question of Lady Macbeth's
children. In Akiro Kurosawa's film adaptation, *Throne of
Blood* (1957), Lady Macbeth tells her husband at the banquet
that she is pregnant, but later miscarries. Writing of her performance in Adrian Noble's 1986 production, Sinead Cusack
observed: 'If you've lost a child and there are no more children, you either leave the man or you become obsessive about
the man and about his happiness and security. That's the ave-
nue I chose to go up as Lady Macbeth' (Rutter, 57). A review
of another production suggests that as Lady Macbeth speaks
of her willingness to kill the child 'you feel the image crosses
[Helen] McCrory's mind and that she has fully grasped what it

is she is saying' (O'Connor, 710). The witches in Philip Franks' 1995 production wheeled an old-fashioned perambulator, and 'the empty pram stays throughout by the stage, a brooding incarnation of a tragedy of childlessness' (O'Connor, 711); the modern *Macbeth on the Estate* (shown on BBC television in 1997) showed images of an empty nursery to suggest grief at a child's death and Andrew Hilton's 2004 production did something similar when Lady Macbeth's sleepwalking had a backdrop of a shrouded cradle and rocking-horse'. Jude Kelly had her Lady Macbeth enter rocking a small toy as if it were a baby: 'as she chops at its little babygro with a pair of scissors, you witness a bereaved mother steeling herself to channel the drive from this terrible lack into the ruthless pursuit of power' (O'Connor, 727); in Rupert Goold's 2008 production, televised and first broadcast in 2010, Lady Macbeth quickly slammed shut a dressing-table drawer in which we glimpse a pair of baby's bootees. A California production directed by Jessica Kubzansky opened with a mimed sequence in which the Macbeths buried their dead child, and Hecate was presented as pregnant. All of these try to make sense of the play's linguistic texture in a literal way, and in doing so, they also work to naturalize Lady Macbeth's own character.

That these recent interpretations of Lady Macbeth's character all seem to focus on her state as a bereaved mother are perhaps the latest attempt to understand, even to rehabilitate, the figure who has most dominated commentary on the play. Dr Johnson wrote that she was 'merely detested' (Johnson, 62). The extent to which she still transgresses norms of female behaviour is striking, although it is also noticeable that, while her behaviour has been dominant in criticism of the play, no one within it, apart from Malcolm in the closing lines, ever expresses any condemnation of her. We might compare the treatment of other forceful, articulate women such as Katherina in *The Taming of the Shrew*, Volumnia in *Coriolanus*, or Paulina in *The Winter's Tale*, all of whose behaviour is subject to negative commentary from other characters in their play. If Shakespeare had wanted to present a stereotypically ambitious woman there were an array of

available tropes from which he could draw, including personal greed, sexual appetite, deceit and hypocrisy: none of
these is present in Lady Macbeth's characterization. Rather,
she is impressively staunch, even heroic: unwavering, putting
her own needs after those of her husband, uncomplaining.
Only her bleak couplets as she awaits Macbeth – is it significant to the state of their relationship by this point that she has
to send a message to her husband via a servant? – give a sense
of her acknowledgement of the cost:

> Nought's had, all's spent,
> Where our desire is got without content:
> 'Tis safer to be that which we destroy,
> Than by destruction dwell in doubtful joy. (3.2.4–7)

That she immediately changes tack when Macbeth enters suggests
that she wants to protect him from her own fears. Shakespeare
may get the image of the warrior woman from Holinshed, who
writes that 'in these days also the women of our country were
of no less courage than the men, for all stout maidens and wives
(if they were not with child) marched well in the field as did
the men'. Perhaps he drew on the edition of Tacitus's Germania
printed in 1604; certainly, strong female roles were prominent
in his writing at this point in his career, probably at least in part
due to the acting capabilities of the King's Men.

Shakespeare represents Lady Macbeth's attainment of the
ruthlessness she desires from the 'Spirits/ That tend on mortal
thoughts' (1.5.39–40) as both unwomanly and unsustainable.
She desires to be unsexed – rid of her femininity and its normative associations of pity and mildness – and Macbeth's admir-
ing, or horrified, 'Bring forth men-children only' (1.7.73) attests
to her management of gender roles: early modern physiology
understood the sex of the unborn child to be determined by
the heat and dryness (qualities identified as masculine) of the
womb. Her own initial response to the murder is briskly practical: 'a little water clears us of this deed' (2.2.66), and it is she
who returns the incriminating daggers to the drunken grooms
when Macbeth bungles their plan and is unable to 'look on't

again' (2.2.51). But she has her own moment of weakness, identifying the patriarch Duncan with her father, and many actors
have identified her fainting at the point when the murder is discovered as a real response to the stress of the situation, rather
than a tactic to cover her husband's verbosity which verges on
evident insincerity. Richard David, reviewing Laurence Olivier
and Vivien Leigh's performances in the 1955 production,
described the way meaning is created from movement:

> Macbeth re-entered from Duncan's room at the opposite
> side and at the back, and began his act, glancing uneasily
> for support to his wife, now divided from him by the whole
> diagonal of the stage. She instinctively took a step forward
> to assist him and, as Macbeth's web of deception grew
> more and more tangled, slowly, inexorably, the two were
> drawn together by the compulsion of their common guilt to
> the centre of the stage. Just before she reached her husband
> Lady Macbeth fainted. Genuine? Feigned? No need even
> to ask the question. Her collapse was an inevitable result
> of the dramatic process as is the spark when two crossed
> wires are brought together. (Kliman, 76)

The faint was important to Sigmund Freud in his essay 'Some
character types met with in Psychoanalytic work'. He offers
Lady Macbeth as 'an example of a person who collapses
on reaching success, after striving for it with single-minded
energy' (Freud, 131). Such an explanation might also be seen
as a return of her repressed femininity, a suggestion of the
difficulty of a woman taking on such unwomanly behaviour.
In the end, this repressed guilt cannot be held off. Her sleepwalking dramatizes a mental breakdown in which the images
and phrases of the night of the murder replay in her restless,
unconscious mind. As her husband becomes hardened to his
crimes, she is shattered by them. Her breakdown thus serves
ironically as a kind of reassurance about gender norms: a
woman cannot really be as diabolical and unfeeling as she
attempts to be. We might see the theatrical consensus about
Lady Macbeth as a grieving or infertile woman in a similar

light: a distinctly female cause is given in explanation and mitigation for behaviour that might otherwise be designated transgressively unfeminine. A woman mourning a lost child can – just – be an object of sympathy. Lady Macbeth's conduct is thus realigned with normative gender roles.

Writing matters

I Character and cue-scripts

Review the discussion of cue-scripts above, and make one to work on the character of Lady Macbeth or of Macduff. How does restricting yourself to the actor's part inform or change the way you see that character? Is there a particular way in which they seem to speak? And how might their cues help them think about the part they are required to play?

II Image clusters

Think about the imagery of disease and sickness and how you might draw that cluster together to discuss the play's themes and plot. What role do the two doctors play in adjacent scenes in England and in Scotland? How might this image cluster touch on the themes of costume and of darkness discussed above?

III Performance

Using material about the play in performance – reviews, material relating to productions, film clips, production photographs – try to set out some of the possibilities for Lady Macbeth's character in the theatre. How might these reflect contemporaneous views of gender roles? How far do they capture the play's nuance?

CHAPTER FOUR

Writing topics

Ten tips for your own writing

1 *Quote, don't paraphrase.* Try to use as much of Shakespeare's language in your writing as you can, since that will avoid you from pre-interpreting it in your own paraphrase. Show how something happens in the play, rather than just stating it as a fact (for example, whether Lady Macbeth 'persuades' her husband to undertake the murder is a matter of interpretation: you could argue it with close reference to the text, but it can't be just assumed).

2 *Use the play's own structure to organize your thoughts.* You don't need to work through the entire play from start to finish, but you can use the end of the play to help conclude your own paper, or the beginning to get started.

3 *Choose an epitomizing scene* as a focus for your investigation, and draw in examples from others more sparingly. This will allow you to focus on the specifics of the language without having to dot around everywhere in the play.

4 *Don't get too bogged down in criticism* and what other people have said. Once you start to think that everything has been said before, you're doomed. The best location for your own thoughts is in detailed analysis of the specifics of a particular speech or scene, rather than in more general and free-floating interpretations.

5 *Use other visualizing techniques* if they work for you: making a diagram of the interactions of the play, or a word cloud of particular imagery, or a graph about who speaks most. It can sometimes be helpful to take the psychologies out of the play and to see it more clearly via numbers or visuals. Experiment with this if it's your thing.

6 *Find a way to talk about multiple meanings.* This book has tried to show that Shakespeare's meaning is always in excess of the context and situation in which language is communicated. This is the surplus that's intrinsic to poetry, or to art – it's what makes art different from everyday life; it's why we wouldn't meet Macbeth in the street, it's why the play is worthy of the kind of attention this book has tried to give it. Get comfortable with words like 'equivocal' and 'ambiguous', and try to make sure that you are writing about the *play's* contradictions rather than being yourself contradictory.

7 *You're not required to find a single answer.* Most questions about Shakespeare are interesting precisely because the play prompts them through its own ambiguities: it's the questions, rather than their answers, that are important. If there weren't unresolved questions, we would have stopped reading and performing these plays long ago. Acknowledge the issues, rather than try to cut through them. If there's something that's difficult to work out, write about the difficulty and how the play produces it (the question of agency discussed in Chapter Three, for instance) rather than trying to sort it out in some mental space outside your writing.

8 *Shakespeare doesn't have a 'message'.* Remember
Hollywood producer Sam Goldwyn's oft-quoted
'Pictures are for entertainment, messages should be
delivered by Western Union?' Shakespeare's plays are
too ambiguous, too messy, simply too *much* (William
Hazlitt's wonderfully over-the-top word for this
over-the-topness was 'supererogatory') to be moral or
political propaganda.

9 *Remember these are plays.* Try to think about the
impact of the lines or scenes or of your argument
about them in performance. Lines can sound
very different if they are delivered with different
intonation, or if the character is in a position of power
or weakness, or if the stage is busy with onlookers or
private and unobserved. Citing examples from specific
productions is absolutely appropriate and scholarly but
(a) don't be vague: identify the date, place and name
of the director; (b) make clear that you recognize that
what these have done is a particular interpretation,
not the play itself; and (c) while you can read about
performances – newspaper reviews online are a good
source, as are production photographs which give
you a sense of the setting and context – you should
also make use of the excellent and divergent canon of
film *Macbeth*s so that you are responding directly to
performance, rather than at one remove.

10 *Don't discount discrepancies.* There's always a
tendency to suppress information that doesn't
quite fit your overall argument, but your writing
will actually be stronger if you acknowledge
counter-examples. Sometimes things that don't fit
are in themselves very significant: for me, the scene
in the play when Macbeth goes on to the murderers
about the different types of dogs is a very odd
moment, and one that I find myself coming back to
as the counter to a lot of my arguments about speed
and compression.

Questions about *Macbeth*

In this short section I take some often-asked questions about *Macbeth*, often taken from message-boards online or from college syllabi. Some of the questions are naive or, at least, can prompt naive answers. My aim here is to point out how the questions can be approached in a more interesting and a more directly linguistic way.

What is the significance of the opening scene of *Macbeth*?

Great question, since this immediately gives us a focal scene (see tip 3 above) from which to begin. We might begin here by looking at the language of the opening scene – its particular rhythm, rhyme and vocabulary, as well as the acoustic and visual effects of thunder and lightning – and how this establishes the mood of the opening. You might want to refer back to the discussion of the witches in Chapter One. Clearly, this is a play which begins, literally, with a bang – a clap of thunder – something that raises the audience heartbeat because it is a shock. Thus the play opens in an atmosphere of suspense and fear, which you might want to discuss as appropriate for what is coming next. The play begins with two scenes in which Macbeth is discussed, shaping our view of the eponymous hero before we meet him ourselves: his implication with these mysterious figures is an interesting part of his pre-entry characterization, particularly compared with the description of his extreme battle valour in 1.2.

Thinking about specific productions would also be useful here. In Polanski's film, for instance, eerie music and the desolate mewing of seagulls over a deserted beach at dawn accompanies the three Weird Sisters. They look like eccentric women of different ages, rather than supernatural forces: one is young, one apparently blind and they drag their possessions on a cart. They dig in the wet sand, conducting a silent ritual including burying a hand holding a knife, and a noose, in the sand, sprinkled with blood as they mutter their spell. As the opening credits roll we hear the clash of metal and the panicked hoofbeat of horses as the battle rages: 1.2 is set on the same stretch of beach, now littered with the dead and half-dead. Orson Welles' opening introduces the witches with words from Act 4, focusing on their preparation of the spell. The camera shows them silhouetted on a craggy rock, but focuses more on the boiling contents of the cauldron from which they shape a human shape they call Macbeth. *Macbeth on the Estate* does not give us any direct equivalent of the play's 1.1, other than the television lottery draw that holds Macbeth's momentary attention as he charges through the home of the rebels. All of these interpretations, and the many others from the history of performance on stage and screen, have something to say about the extent to which the Weird Sisters are powerful. Their plan to meet Macbeth raises the question of how far they control, and how far they merely foresee, events in the play – discussed in more detail in Chapter Three. This question has a profound impact on how we see the characters of the play, particularly Macbeth himself, and while it's a question that directors and critics attempt to answer with certainty, it seems more fruitful, and more true to the experience of the play, to present it as something unresolved in the text, a gap awaiting our collaboration.

Is *Macbeth* a moral play?

This is the kind of question that looks as if it requires yes or no. Probably trying to resist that absolute binary would be a helpful strategy for bringing out the play's ambiguities (see tips 6, 7 and 8 above). A more sophisticated answer to any of these 'closed' type questions always raises the points on both sides of the argument, and might, but needn't necessarily seek to adjudicate them. For ease here I'll suggest some arguments for and against: you might want to structure a written answer in a more interconnected way than this outline.

For the play being moral: we might think about the presentation of Duncan and the way his murder sets natural order into chaos, as the Old Man and Ross discuss in 2.4. Darkness, associated with the Macbeths' soliloquies in Act 1, is replaced in the final act by a light associated with Malcolm, just as natural images of growth associated with Duncan return with Malcolm's use of the word 'planted' in his final speech. These linguistic patterns suggest that the rightful succession has been restored. You might look to the play's rewriting of the historical record as found in Holinshed's *Chronicles*: in his purposive changes to the depiction of Duncan and of Macbeth, Shakespeare has designed a story about regicide as a terrible crime, rather than the expedient political strategy it seems to be in the sources. He has cut evidence that Macbeth was a successful ruler, making his reign one of terror and darkness. Macbeth's own description of the consequences of murdering the king in his soliloquy in 1.7 (look back to Chapter One to refamiliarize yourself with that discussion) does seem to be realized in the play. There is no rest, no pity, no sleep, no return. Macbeth has 'put rancours in the vessel of my peace': the play shows how he is haunted – in the banquet scene, literally – by his misdeeds. Finally, when the man whose family's blood is on his hands kills him, Macbeth gets the appropriate punishment for his crimes. On the other side, we might suggest that the play, written for a commercial audience, is required to be entertaining rather than didactic. In showing us the inside of Macbeth's troubled intelligence, the play makes us sympathize with him; we saw that in its depiction of Malcolm, particularly in 4.3, the play withholds fully endorsing him as a fit successor (and productions, which you might want to cite here, often emphasize the extent to which his rule may be similar to, rather than the opposite of, his predecessor). In giving us a summary of the Macbeths that seems to understate their complexity, the play's final lines open up a question about them rather than providing a conclusive moral digest. If you feel setting out the case for and against seems to leave the issue hanging in a way that is uncommitted rather than delicately balanced, you could reshape the question to attach the answer to a particular production. Is Polanski's *Macbeth* moral? Is Goold's?

Describe how Lady Macbeth persuades Macbeth to commit murder

This is a question I think I'd attack at the root, since it's a presupposition to start with. *Does* Lady Macbeth persuade Macbeth to murder? That is a real question. The focal scene here has to be 1.7, and you might want to draw on 1.5 too: it's worth remembering from the start that the later scenes in which Lady Macbeth urges, taunts or variously tries to assert power over Macbeth post-date the murder of Duncan. Thinking carefully about the linguistic evidence from the couple's first meeting in the play (have a look back at Harriet Walter's compelling account of how she and Antony Sher understood the exchange in 1.5, on pages 132–3) may suggest that both partners have already thought about the deed without explicitly articulating it (you might want to go back to Macbeth's own initial response to the prediction and his asides in 1.4, and to Lady Macbeth's soliloquy earlier in this scene when she receives Macbeth's letter). In 1.7, an analysis of Macbeth's incomplete soliloquy is itself inconclusive: is he at the point of persuading himself away from the murder, or simply wavering and likely to come back to it, as he has done already in a speech studded with 'but'? How do you interpret his final, confused metaphor of vaulting: and what is 'th'other' with which it ends? What do you think of Macbeth's speech which begins 'We will proceed no further in this business': are his lines here the strongest counterclaim to regicide that he could be expected to make at this point, or are they a rather weak interjection which is almost asking to be over-ruled?

Some actors might think that in ending on an incomplete
verse line 'Not cast aside so soon', Macbeth metrically, and
thus psychologically, invites his wife to countermand him: he
has left his argument vulnerable, and perhaps deliberately.

Looking in some detail at the language of gender in the
scene would give some insight into the roles of the two protagonists: ideas of 'man' are distinguished against 'woman'
on the one hand and 'beast' on the other. Your argument
might need to have some analysis of Lady Macbeth's most
horrific simile, about dashing the brains from 'the babe that
milks me', and of the different performance possibilities of
'We fail' (see Chapter Three for discussion). It may be from
this analysis that your argument proceeds as an amplified version of something like – Lady Macbeth persuades Macbeth
to murder by taunting him over his masculinity – supported,
of course, by close textual reference. Or it may be that you
feel Lady Macbeth does not really persuade him at all, and
that the language reveals a Macbeth who relies on his wife to
affirm and intuit his own desires, or who has already decided
that he will become king through murder, or who is controlled by quite different external forces such as the witches. So
behind the 'how' of the question there are appropriate prior
questions: unpicking the fact that the assumptions of a question are just that, assumptions, can be liberating, and, so long
as your argument is impeccably supported with textual evidence, should be relatively uncontroversial.

How does Shakespeare use the theme of appearance versus reality in *Macbeth*?

'Appearance and reality' is a real old chestnut of Shakespeare
studies and one which, like the sailor's wife in 1.3, critics are
unwilling to give up. It can be a useful way to conceptual-
ize a gap between the way things seem and how they really

are. Lady Macbeth's instruction that her husband should 'look like th'innocent flower/ But be the serpent under't' is a strategic deployment of the theme: Macbeth must pretend to be something he is not. The play goes on to explore whether appearances are real at moments such as Duncan's ingenous 'There's no art/ To find the mind's construction in the face', or Macbeth's own sceptical 'Is this a dagger which I see before me', when he explores the possibility that what he sees is 'a false creation/ Proceeding from the heat-oppressed brain'. Thinking about these and other examples will help to trace the opposition between how things look and how they really are throughout the play.

But I think there is some more sophisticated work to do with this question. What adherents of the 'appearance/reality' dichotomy do not often acknowledge is that the theatre is a somewhat inadequate place to explore the binary, since even 'reality' in the theatre is actually 'appearance', men in costume and role, acting on a stage. The habitual self-consciousness of the theatre of Shakespeare's time means that it does not seem to want us to forget this fact: Coleridge's famous phrase about art requiring our 'willing suspension of disbelief' has often been applied to Shakespeare, but the role of the audience at an early modern play is more complicated than that. Plays were performed in daylight with relatively few props and spectators must have been as aware of other audience members as they were of the players (pictures of the rebuilt Globe Theatre on London's Bankside give a modern version of this proximity and consciousness): speeches tended to be spoken out to the audience in recognition that they were there (rather than maintaining what has been called a 'fourth wall' separating the stage from the audience, and which is a consequence of more modern theatre designs). There may well have been more improvisation and interaction between stage and yard. So, at least at some points in the performance, audiences are required to register that what they are seeing is illusory. Some of the pleasure of special effects, of which this play, with its sequence of illusions and magical conjurations, is full, is always to try to understand how they are done. Visual effects on stage thus contribute to the illusion of realism and simultaneously reveal it as constructed: they prompt both wonder and scepticism. When Macbeth likens the emptiness of life to 'a poor player/ That struts and frets his hour upon the stage,/ And then is heard no more', only moments before the end of the play and of his part, the pleasure for the audience must have been in recognizing that Macbeth draws on a metaphor (appearance) which is in fact true (reality): he *is* a poor player, we are in a theatre. The gap between appearance and reality seems to lose its ethical clarity and its critical purchase.

What is the purpose of the porter scene?

Another question with a direct focal scene, inviting us to connect it, structurally and thematically, with the rest of the play. Although 'purpose' suggests a single answer, you are probably going to want to give multiple reasons. Start by reviewing the scene closely, and reminding yourself of the scene immediately before (the confused and tense passage in which Macbeth returns to his chamber mistakenly bringing the bloodied daggers) and what happens afterwards (the scene develops into the shocked discovery of Duncan's murder). You will probably see immediately that the scene is a contrast from the edgy conference before (see Chapter Three for an analysis of Macbeth and Lady Macbeth here) and the terrible revelation afterwards. The Porter speaks in a grumbling prose, half cheerful, half grudging, as he answers the urgent night-time knocking on the castle door: it is a language quite different from the highly wrought emotional register on either side of it. This recognition might help you develop some plot or dramaturgical purposes to the scene in managing the stress and mood of the play at this point. Some critics use the idea of 'comic relief' to explain this as a paradox of heightening tension by alleviating it.

If part of the answer to the question will involve ideas of contrast, another will probably develop lines of continuity. Look at the Porter's speech and his reference to 'devil-porter' and 'porter of Hell-gate' – what does this metaphor do to Macbeth's castle (and might Seyton/'Satan' become relevant also)? His joking riff on the ill-effects of drink on sexual performance is a parodic version of the narrowing gap between desire and execution discussed in Chapter Two. The introduction discusses the contemporary importance of ideas of equivocation in the aftermath of the Gunpowder Plot: being topical might be one of the purposes here, and the notion also connects the scene to the witches' riddling words. On the topicality point you might want to consider modern performances of this scene. Often it has been rewritten sometimes as a modern political monologue, so that the comedy works anew, since the verbal humour and in-jokes we get here tend to be rather obscure to modern audiences. So a number of purposes present themselves: dramatic, topical, humorous, connected to the wider themes of the play – and that's before we get to the practical point that Macbeth needs some time to clean his bloody hands before making a plausible entrance as the sleeping householder roused to bear witness to a terrible crime. The job of your written analysis is to give them some sort of logical order: from most important to least, perhaps, or grouped under different headings so that you look at the dramatic purposes first, say, and then at how the scene connects to the play's wider concerns.

Writing skills review

The proposed material for all of these questions tries to reinstate close linguistic analysis as the foundation of writing about *Macbeth*. As we have seen, that does not at all mean that you cannot write about character or about plot or about performance; rather, that it is important to see all these elements as linguistically constructed. Quoting extensively from the play gives your own prose the wonderful texture of Shakespeare's own writing: thinking about appropriate phrases and even single significant words as quotations within your own sentences gives authority and poetry to your analysis. As Macbeth comes to realize about the witches' false comforts, the devil – and the beauty – is in the detail. *Macbeth* is not *about*, it *is*. This book has tried to open that up.

BIBLIOGRAPHY AND FURTHER READING

Bibliography

Adelman, Janet, *Suffocating Mothers: Fantasies of Maternal Origin Shakespeare's Plays, 'Hamlet' to 'The Tempest'* (New York and London, Routledge, 1992).

Austin, J. L., *How to Do Things with Words* (Oxford, Clarendon Press, 1962).

Barroll, J. Leeds, *Politics, Plague and Shakespeare's Theatre* (Ithaca, Cornell University Press, 1991).

Barton, John, *Playing Shakespeare* (London, Methuen, 1984).

Bate, Jonathan and Eric Rasmussen (eds), *The RSC Shakespeare* (London, Macmillan, 2007).

Bate, Jonathan, *The Romantics on Shakespeare* (Harmondsworth, Penguin, 1992).

Beckett, Samuel, *Our Exagmination Round His Factification for Incamination of Work in Progress* (London, Faber, 1929).

Berger, Harry Jr, 'The Early Scenes of *Macbeth*: A Preface to a New Interpretation', *English Literary History* 47 (1980), 1–31.

Berry, Cicely, *The Actor and His Text* (London, 1987).

Bradley, A. C., *Shakespearean Tragedy* (1904; Basingstoke, 1986).

Braunmuller, A. R. (ed.), *Macbeth: The New Cambridge Shakespeare* (Cambridge, 2008).

Brooke, Nicholas (ed.), *Macbeth* (Oxford, 1990).

Brooks, Cleanth, *The Well-Wrought Urn: Studies in the Structure of Poetry* (London, Dobson, 1949).

Crystal, David, *Think on My Words: Exploring Shakespeare's Language* (Cambridge, Cambridge University Press, 2008).

de Grazia, Margreta and Peter Stallybrass, 'The Materiality of the Shakespearean Text', *Shakespeare Quarterly* 44 (1993), 255–83.

De Quincey, Thomas, 'On the Knocking at the Gate in *Macbeth*', in John Wain (ed.), *Macbeth: A Casebook* (London and Basingstoke, Macmillan, 1968), 90–96.

Dillon, Janette, *The Cambridge Introduction to Shakespeare's Tragedies* (Cambridge, Cambridge University Press, 2007).

Dobson, Michael, *Performing Shakespeare's Tragedies Today: The Actor's Perspective* (Cambridge, 2006).

Eagleton, Terry, *William Shakespeare* (Oxford, Basil Blackwell, 1986).

Evans, Malcolm, *Signifying Nothing: Truth's True Contents in Shakespeare's Text* (Brighton, Harvester Wheatsheaf, 1986).

Freud, Sigmund, 'Some Character Types Met with in Psycho-analytic Work', in John Wain (ed.), *Macbeth: A Casebook* (London, Macmillan, 1968), 131–8.

Furness, H. H. (ed.), *Macbeth* (Lippincott, Philadelphia, 1873).

Garber, Marjorie, *Shakespeare After All* (New York, Pantheon Books, 2004).

Goldman, Michael, *Acting and Action in Shakespearean Tragedy* (Princeton, Princeton University Press, 1985).

Greenblatt, Stephen, *Will in the World: How Shakespeare Became Shakespeare* (London, Jonathan Cape, 2004).

Greenblatt, Stephen, Walter Cohen, Jean E. Howard and Katharine Eisaman Maus (eds), *The Norton Shakespeare* (2nd edn; New York and London, 2008).

Donaldson, Ian (ed.), *The Oxford Authors: Ben Jonson* (Oxford, Oxford University Press, 1985).

Ionesco, Eugene, *Plays,* Vol. 9, trans. Donald Watson (London, Calder and Boyars, 1973).

Jacobi, Derek, 'Macbeth', in R. L. Smallwood (ed.), *Players of Shakespeare 4* (Cambridge, Cambridge University Press, 1998), 193–210.

Johnson, Samuel, 'Comments on *Macbeth*', in John Wain (ed.), *Macbeth: A Casebook* (Macmillan, London and Basingstoke, 1968), 49–62.

Jones, Emrys, *Scenic Form in Shakespeare* (Oxford, Clarendon Press, 1971).

Kahn, Coppélia, *Man's Estate: Masculine Identity in Shakespeare* (Berkeley, University of California Press, 1981).

Kermode, Frank, *Shakespeare's Language* (London, Allen Lane, 2000).

Kliman, Bernice W., *Macbeth: Shakespeare in Performance* (Manchester, Manchester University Press, 1992).

Knights, L. C., 'How many Children Had Lady Macbeth?' in *Explorations* (Harmondsworth, Penguin, 1946), 15–54.

Kott, Jan, *Shakespeare Our Contemporary* (London, Routledge, 1967).

Maguire, Laurie and Emma Smith, *Thirty Great Myths about Shakespeare* (Oxford, Wiley-Blackwell, 2012).

McLuskie, Kathleen E., *Macbeth: Writers and their Work* (Horndon, Northcote House, 2007).

Merton, R. K., *Social Theory and Social Structure* (2nd edn; New York, Free Press, 1968).

Miller, Arthur, *The Crucible* (Penguin, Harmondsworth, 1968).

Muir, Kenneth (ed.), *Macbeth: The Arden Shakespeare* (London, Arden Shakespeare, 2001).

O'Connor, John and Katharine Goodland, *A Directory of Shakespeare in Performance: 1970–2005*, Vol. 1 (Basingstoke, Palgrave Macmillan, 2007).

Orlin, Lena Cowen, 'Domestic Tragedy: Private Life on the Public Stage', in Arthur F. Kinney (ed.), *A Companion to Renaissance Drama* (Oxford, Blackwell Publishers, 2002), 367–83.

Out of Joint, 'Education Notes for Out of Joint "Macbeth" Programme', www.outofjoint.co.uk/wp-content/uploads/2010/09/Mac_pac1.doc.

Palfrey, Simon and Tiffany Stern, *Shakespeare in Parts* (Oxford, Clarendon Press, 2007).

Palfrey, Simon, *Doing Shakespeare* (2nd edn; London, Arden Shakespeare, 2011).

Popper, Karl, *The Poverty of Historicism* (London, Routledge and Kegan Paul, 1974), 13.

Purkiss, Diane, *The Witch in History: Early Modern and Twentieth Century Representations* (London, Routledge, 1996).

Radcliffe, Ann, 'On the Supernatural in Poetry', www.litgothic.com/Texts/radcliffe_sup.pdf

Rodenburg, Patsy, *The Actor Speaks: Voice and the Performer* (London, 1988).

— *Speaking Shakespeare* (London, Methuen, 2002).

Rutter, Carol, *Clamorous Voices: Shakespeare's Women Today* (London, The Women's Press, 1988).

Sidney, Philip, 'The Defence of Poesy', in Katherine Duncan-Jones (ed.), *The Oxford Authors: Sir Philip Sidney*, (Oxford, Oxford University Press, 1991), 212–51.

Smith, Emma, 'Shakespeare and Early Modern Tragedy', in Emma
    Smith and Garrett E. Sullivan (eds), *The Cambridge Companion
    to English Renaissance Tragedy* (Cambridge, Cambridge
    University Press, 2010), 132–49.
Spurgeon, Caroline, *Shakespeare's Imagery: And what It Tells Us*
    (Cambridge, Cambridge University Press, 1935).
Tanner, Tony, *Prefaces to Shakespeare* (Cambridge, MA: Belknap
    Press, 2010).
Taylor, Gary and John Lavagnino (eds), *Thomas Middleton:
    The Collected Works* (Oxford, Clarendon Press, 2007).
Wain, John (ed.), *Macbeth: A Casebook* (London, Macmillan,
    1968).
Walter, Harriet, *Macbeth* (London, Faber, 2002).
Wilders, John, *Shakespeare in Production: Macbeth* (Cambridge,
    Cambridge University Press, 2004).
Wills, Garry, *Witches and Jesuits: Shakespeare's Macbeth*
    (New York and Oxford, Oxford University Press, 1995).
Wilson, John Dover (ed.), *Macbeth* (Cambridge, Cambridge
    University Press, 1947).

Further reading, viewing and browsing

Criticism

The aim of this book has been to encourage you to read Shakespeare
closely for yourself, rather than to lose your own voice among the
thousands of critical texts out there. With a firm basis in the text –
with all its complexities and ambiguities – you are in a good position
to read other critical views and set your own thoughts against them.
The references above are all recommended works. Here are a few
other directions to take.

On the history of criticism, look at Nicolas Tredell, *Macbeth*
(*Readers' Guides to Essential Criticism*: Basingstoke, Macmillan,
2006), which gives extensive quotation from critics over the last
400 years, plus informed commentary. Two collections of essays
review some of the more recent critical work: Alan Sinfield's *New*

Casebooks: Macbeth (Basingstoke, Macmillan, 1992) and Samuel Schoenbaum's *Macbeth: Critical Essays* (New York and London, Garland, 1991). Tiffany Stern's *Making Shakespeare: From Stage to Page* (London, Routledge, 2004) makes some stimulating connections between the plays and the theatres for which they were written; James Shapiro's *1599: A Year in the Life of Shakespeare* (London, Faber, 2005) focuses on the local connections between history and theatre (look out for his next book which does the same for the year 1606). Lois Potter's biography of Shakespeare (Oxford, Wiley-Blackwell, 2012) avoids too much speculation about the man and instead interrogates the plays in the context of early modern theatre. *The New Cambridge Companion to Shakespeare* (Cambridge, Cambridge University Press, 2010), edited by Margreta de Grazia and Stanley Wells, ranges over different methodological approaches and gives extensive suggestions for further reading.

For thinking more generally about literary study, I warmly recommend Andrew Bennett and Nicholas Royle's *An Introduction to Literature, Criticism and Theory* (Basingstoke, Macmillan, 2009). And for thinking about your own writing, try Sylvan Barnet and William E. Cain, *A Short Guide to Writing about Literature* (10th edn; New York, Longman, 2005), the classic *The Elements of Style* by William Strunk Jr and E. B. White (4th edn; New York, Longman, 1999) or John R. Trimble's *Writing with Style* (3rd edn; London, Longman, 2010).

Films

There are major films of *Macbeth* by Orson Welles (1948) and Roman Polanski (1971). There are television versions of stage productions by Trevor Nunn (1979), Penny Woolcock (*Macbeth on the Estate*, 1997) and Rupert Goold (2010), as well as a made-for-television version by Jack Gold (1983). Film adaptations include *Scotland Pa* (dir. Billy Morrisette, 2001), *Men of Respect* (dir. William Reilly, 1990) and *Throne of Blood* (dir. Akira Kurosawa, 1957). For more details, see the Internet Movie Database at http://imdb.com.

Websites

- Internet Shakespeare Editions, University of Victoria
    http://internetshakespeare.uvic.ca/
    Lots of materials, including a transcribed, unmodernized
    Folio text of *Macbeth* linked to a digital facsimile of the
    book.

- Bodleian Library First Folio
    http://shakespeare.bodleian.ox.ac.uk
    Important digitized version of a copy of the First Folio in
    its original condition.

- Shakespeare's Words
    http://shakespeareswords.com/
    Site including glossaries and searchable full text, put
    together by David Crystal, the foremost expert on
    Shakespeare's language.

- Approaching Shakespeare
    http://podcasts.ox.ac.uk
    My free lectures on Shakespeare's plays, designed for
    students at the University of Oxford.

- The Holinshed Project
    http://www.cems.ox.ac.uk/holinshed/
    Read the text of Shakespeare's source.